SILVER BOXES

In memory of my Mother.

SILVER BOXES

Eric Delieb

Photographs by
Michael Plomer

 Clarkson N. Potter, Inc.
Publisher **NEW YORK**

Produced by Design Yearbook Limited, 21 Ivor Place, London N.W.1.
Published by Clarkson N. Potter, Inc., 419 Park Avenue South, New York,
N.Y. 10016.
Text set by Yendall & Company Limited, Riscatype House, 22/25 Red
Lion Court, Fleet Street, London E.C.4.
Colour origination by Supreme Litho Limited, 77/79 Parkway, Camden
Town, London N.W.1.
Printed by L. Van Leer & Company N.V. of Amsterdam.
Bound by Nevett, Key & Whiting Limited, The Hyde, Colindale, London
N.W.9.

Art Director: Ian Cameron.
House Editor and Designer: Tom Carter.

Printed in Holland and bound in England.

Library of Congress Catalog Card No. 68-31838

CONTENTS

The writer wishes to express his deep indebtedness to the anonymous collectors who kindly permitted him to illustrate articles from their collections and to the following for kind advice and technical assistance:

The Worshipful Company of Barbers and J. H. L. Trustram, Esq., MBE, MA, the Clerk and Solicitor.

The Birmingham Assay Office: H. A. Westwood, Esq., Assay Master, Miss D. E. Dudley, Secretary to the Assay Master,
A. Cartland, Esq., Warden, Assay Office,
Michael Roberts, Esq., Photographic Records Department.

Birmingham Central Reference Library: Miss D. McCulla and Miss D. N. Norris, and the staff of the Local Studies Library.

H. E. Brocksom, Esq.

Mrs. Shirley Bury, Victoria and Albert Museum.

Miss M. E. Cliff.

Edward Croft-Murray, Esq., MBE, Keeper of the Department of Prints and Drawings, British Museum.

Rev. R. Dunwell, Rector, St. Peter's Church, Cogenhoe, Northamptonshire.

Messrs. William R. Fletcher and Keith R. Fletcher.

Monseigneur R. J. Foster, Rector of St. Mary's College, Oscott, Warwickshire and Mr. Thomas Fenwick, Sacrist.

The Board of General Purposes, Freemasons' Hall, and A. R. Hewitt, Esq., Librarian and Curator, and John Groves, Esq., Assistant Curator, Grand Lodge Museum, Freemasons' Hall, London, W.C.2.

L. H. Gilbert Esq.

The Wardens of the Worshipful Company of Goldsmiths and Miss Susan Hare, Librarian to the Company.

Rev. W. A. Hepher, MA.

Mrs. G. E. P. How.

Messrs. Victor Joliffe and William Hathaway, of Messrs. Brown & Co., Birmingham.

Derek Keen, Esq.

E. Kish, Esq.

F. L. Lancaster, Esq., of Messrs. G. H. Lancaster, Ltd., Birmingham.

Mrs. Beryl Linwood of Sandringham, Victoria, Australia, and the late Charles Linwood, Esq.

Mrs. J. S. Martin of the Department of Coins and Medals, British Museum.

O. T. Miles, Esq.

Dr. George Mitchell.

Maurice Newbold, Esq.

Charles C. Oman, Esq.

H. Rubin, Esq.

Richard F. H. Vander, Esq.

The Trustees of the Wellcome Medical Historical Museum and J. K. Crellyn Esq., Curator, and Robin Price, Esq., Assistant Librarian.

The photographs of the enlarged Birmingham Makers Marks appended to the Genealogical sections are by Michael Roberts of the Photographic Records Department, Birmingham Assay Office.

With the exception of those on pages 50 and 76, which are by Peter Parkinson, AIBP, and that on page 40, by Otto Auer of Lisbon, all the colour photographs are by Michael Plomer.

Preface

This book is based, in the main, upon a thesis of my own development, namely, that any receptacle which has a lid, attached or not, and which was intended to accommodate articles other than victuals (which would make it a 'vessel') may be grouped under the general heading of 'box'. Thus the famous and wholly beautiful Henry VIII (some say Henry VII) 'Barber Surgeons' Case' with its superb engravings and wonderfully coloured enamels, is as much a 'box' as any snuffbox or vinaigrette produced in Birmingham some three and a half centuries later. Taking this argument a step further, I have deliberately introduced what I term 'special-purpose boxes', that is, boxes which were intended, from the very beginning, to serve a specific function. One enchanting item illustrated is a little artists' colour-box, or paintbox, another a superlative combination tobacco-box cum pipebox, with lids opening on all sides, and yet a third, a charmingly austere Commonwealth sweetmeat box—all are boxes, but of diverse forms and functions.

I have been fortunate enough to be able to call upon the collections of some of Britain's premier connoisseurs, as well as of five distinguished Livery and Museum collections, and have carefully selected only the most unusual types and those by the finest makers. Indeed, so painstakingly meticulous has this selection been, that many excellent examples were discarded. What is more, having already written and illustrated a very full chapter on the subject of 'The Box' in my last book, *Investing in Silver*, I did not wish to cover the same ground again, and thus various aspects are not discussed in this work.

I have also been favoured with the utmost co-operation of the acknowledged experts in this field, and this book could never have been written at all, were it not for the exceptionally deep interest which all my helpers displayed throughout. I record my deep appreciation to these elsewhere, but one outstanding source of information must be acknowledged here: I refer to Mr. Hamil Westwood, the Assay Master and his devoted staff at the Birmingham Assay Office. There poured from Birmingham an absolute avalanche of detailed information which, when analysed and arranged, opens up completely new vistas upon subjects hitherto veiled and shrouded in enigma. I have been able to complete five complicated genealogies of the leading Birmingham boxmakers, but, in keeping with the remainder of the work, have endeavoured to keep the technical data at a minimum, so as to make the book readable. I therefore do not illustrate elaborate genealogical tables and 'Family Trees', but simply give the details in the text.

There are, in this work, three main objectives: to make the subject interesting, to make it entertaining, and to cover those nebulous subjects which other writers, either through neglect or deliberate intent have omitted to discuss. I have therefore devoted the whole of the third chapter to a long and penetrating, but not, I hope, confusing, analysis of 'Applied Ornament' on boxes, and have introduced a newly conceived concept, which, in my opinion, constitutes an entirely novel approach to the subject, and which, I trust, succeeds in giving it a fresh 'dimension'.

Following the example of my last book, I have attempted to introduce newly uncovered and unusual material, and have reconstructed various historical episodes of otherwise somewhat vague form. My attention, however, has been focused more on technical developments than in early origins, and I have thus devoted myself to a deep study of the former, which include such topics as bright-cutting, engine-turning and engraving, which are normally referred to only in passing. Other methods involved in 'Applied Ornament' have been subjected to a 'comparative analysis', with startling results, in which examination I was greatly aided by a senior Birmingham craftsman who is one of the few remaining specialists in his field.

It should be stated that the illustrations come from the collections of English specialists only, but that, either through modesty or prudence, chiefly the former, they have elected to remain anonymous. This of course excludes the Livery Companies and Museums which have adequate security arrangements and can thus be named with impunity.

Finally, I hope that this work will bring to collector and book-lover alike a new appreciation of the genus 'box'. This versatile article, which is of so many differing forms, and has so many diverse uses, has many ardent admirers, among whom I am honoured to be, but that is not my reason for writing this book. It was a marathon task, but one which I accepted gladly, if only to do adequate justice to those wonderful craftsmen who had been anonymous for so long, because no one cared sufficiently about their work to undertake a searching review of their masterpieces. I hope that this mission has been successful and that this researched work will prove as absorbing to read as it was to write.

1. Special Purpose Boxes

What is a box? Certainly it is a receptacle with a lid, hinged or otherwise. The shape matters little, but the function of the article is all-important. On the point of etymology lexicographers tend to disagree. Some, like Dr. Johnson, distinguish the 'box' from the 'chest', as 'the less from the greater'—he supplies a quotation from Sir Philip Sidney's *Arcadia* (*circa* 1586)—'a magnet, though put in an ivory box, will, through the box, send forth his embracing virtue to a beloved needle'. Others, notably Bartholomew de Glanville (*circa* 1360) define the term as originating with the material from which, at that time, boxes were usually made, the wood of the box-tree (*Buxum Sempervirens*). He mentions, in passing, other uses for the box than as a mere receptacle 'also of boxe that boxes made to kepe in musk and other spicerye'.

The more logical origin for the term is the Greek πύξις a pyx, from the Christian practice of using a consecrated wafer in the communion service as a symbol of the body of Christ. The thread of religious persecution which runs through English History, often inspired by the whims of monarchs, has served to bond many Roman Catholics to their faith, and thus historical references abound which indicate the wide use of the pyx from the earliest times.

Both Ranulf Higden, a Benedictine monk of Chester, author of the famous 'History' of his time (*circa* 1299-1363), the *Polychronicon*, and John Bale, who was a bitter enemy of the Monastic system, and was known as 'Bilious Bale' for his vicious writings against the monks (among them *The Actes of the Englysh Votaryes, comprehending their vnchast practices . . . Reade but laugh not . . .*, [*circa* 1495-1563]) relate of King Stephen's Coronation that 'the pyx in which the sacrament was contende, brekynge the chene, did falle, which was a prognostication contrary to the victory of the kynge' (Trevisa's translation) and, 'they tell of kynge Stuen, that the pixte fell out of hys tabernacle, at his coronacion' (Bale).

Pyxes were widely used in Monasteries: an inventory of 1536 (the year in which the Henry VIII Act was passed for the dissolution of the lesser monasteries) contains '190 Divers Pyxides of Ivory (another version lists 'one pyx evere') with clasps and without them, of silver, with many relicks'. The Inventories of Church Goods for the Counties of York, Durham and Northumberland cite various pyxes which were similarly impounded, and one item entered in an inventory at Hunmanbie, in the East York Riding in 1552 states: 'This bill indented, maid the xvjth daie of August, 6 Edward VI: Item: 1 pyx of silver'. The Act of 1536 gave to Henry VIII the ornaments, jewels, goods and chattels of such foundations, and although it was not specifically mentioned in the Act of 1539 for dissolving the greater monasteries, their goods were also undoubtedly seized under it.

As a result of this legalised robbery, much important sacramental plate was melted down, and very few authentic English boxes (pyxes, caskets and the like) of pre-Reformation times survive. There may well be a few in private possession, but Charles Oman in his *English Church Plate* 597-1830 (OUP, 1957) cites only five. As this important work is the latest comprehensive evaluation of the subject, this figure is likely to be correct. The most impressive of Mr. Oman's illustrations is the superb gold pyx at Westminster Cathedral, but as this present work is dedicated to the study of the 'English *Silver* Box', it was decided to restrict illustrations to those boxes made in silver and silver-gilt. Thus, three specimens are shown: two of early provenance, and one in Pugin's 'Mediaeval Revival' style.

At this juncture, it ought to be pointed out that there are many foreign pyxes extant, in Limoges Champlevé Enamels, bronzes, and copper-gilt, but these escaped the Reformation, or were possibly imported as substitutes. The reason that the English pyx has been elected to open this survey of English Silver Boxes is that it is the earliest surviving silver receptacle of actual 'box-form'.

Of the two early pyxes shown, the circular example is the more interesting: it is of undoubted English origin, and bears the scratched date '1649' and the owner's initials 'IM' on the back. It is a simple little box, engraved on the lid with a band of arabesque foliate motifs, interspersed with primitive Tudor Roses. Engraved within this band are the Sacred Monogram and Heart pierced with Nails. There is a primitive five-lugged hinge, and a loop, which perhaps engaged upon a hook or other type of fastener. The inside of the box was left 'unplanished', that is, it was not polished, and was permitted to retain the 'flaws' often found in unwrought silver. Obviously, there are no hall-marks—the Puritans' reaction to a communicant's application would have been unpleasant, to say the least!

Notwithstanding his haste to finish the box, however, the unknown silversmith found time to fashion a band of 'reeding' enrichment around the rim.

The second pyx is somewhat later in date, being *circa* 1660, although it is completely undated and unsigned. The front bears an engraved crucifix with the Sacred Legend 'In Hoc Signo Vinces' (Constantine the Great's watchword—'In this Sign shalt thou conquer') and the back with the Agnus Dei motif, and the Sacred Legend 'Ecce Agnus Dei'. The Agnus Dei, of course, symbolises Christ as the 'Lamb of God'. The shape is slightly oval, and the lid has a five-lugged hinge and a suspensory loop, so that it was probably intended for use by an itinerant celebrant. The rim is 'wriggle-engraved' and there is a band of twisted wire gadroon enrichment around the body, probably to serve as a strengthener.

Finally, there is Pugin's beautiful silver-gilt pyx: this is much larger than the other specimens, being probably intended for ceremonial use at St. Mary's Roman Catholic College, at Oscott, near Birmingham. Augustus Welby Northmore Pugin, son of a French architect who had worked for Nash, George IV's famous protegé, was converted to Roman Catholicism in 1834, and his 'neo-Gothic' designs attracted the attentions of Bertram Arthur, 17th earl of Shrewsbury, himself a Catholic and a great patron of St. Mary's, Oscott. Under his patronage, Pugin designed and 'Gothicised' much of the College, and eventually collaborated with the Birmingham craftsman (originally a stained-glass manufacturer) John Hardman. This silver-gilt pyx is a product of their joint design: Pugin provided the 'neo-Gothic' influence, complete with fleurs-de-lys and Gothic characters for the Sacred Monogram, and Hardman made the article in 1849.

The pyx is engraved on the front with the Crucifixion and Sorrowing Angels, and the Agnus Dei is placed within a cartouche surrounded by a band of matt-chased and engraved fleurs-de-lys, and this, in turn, is encircled with a band of neo-Gothic floral motifs on an engraved ground. Pugin and Hardman collaborated to create the 'Mediaeval Court' at the Great Exhibition of 1851, and

Above
Commonwealth Pyx: formed as circular box, reeded around rim, and engraved on lid with arabesque foliate motifs and interspersed with primitively engraved Tudor roses. Engraved inside the circular cartouche with The Sacred Monogram and Sacred Heart pierced with Nails. Five-lugged hinge, and a loop which possibly originally engaged in fastener or hook. The inside of the box not planished, revealing flaws in the metal. Scratched on back with contemporary initials 'IM' and the date '1649'. Unmarked, *circa* 1635-49, probably the latter date, although Charles Oman in his *English Church Plate 597-1830* inclines to the former on stylistic grounds. Size: 2 inches in diameter by 1 inch deep.
By courtesy of Monseigneur R. J. Foster, Rector of St. Mary's College, Oscott, Warwickshire.

Below
Small Charles II Pyx: of oval shape, primitively engraved in contemporary characters. The back with 'Ecce Agnus Dei' and with similar ecclesiastical 'Lamb with Flag' motif, the lid (not shown) engraved 'In Hoc Signo Vinces'. With five-lugged hinge and suspensory loop. The rim 'wriggle-engraved' and enriched with twisted-wire cable-gadroon circlet, and with 'hook' fastener. Unmarked or dated, but thought to be *circa* 1660. Size: 1⅜ inches in diameter by ¾ of an inch deep.
By courtesy of Monseigneur R. J. Foster, Rector of St. Mary's College, Oscott, Warwickshire.

received great praise for their reintroduction of mediaeval designs and methods. The firm of Hardman & Co. is still active in Birmingham at the present day.

One essential constituent of 'dry sweetmeats' (as Samuel Johnson epitomises the group) was a natural dulcifier, and, of course, natural honey was the purest of these: in Anglo-Saxon times, honey was widely used and the wild honey found in the English woods became an article of importance in the Forest Charter (Carta de Foresta—hotly contested common law and forest law rights were among the grievances which united the barons and the people against King John). It would appear, from contemporary records, that the existence of this natural product was the reason why sugar was not brought to England until the 15th century, in any great bulk.

Sugar was at first regarded as a spice, and was introduced as a substitute for honey after the Crusades (there is a contemporary record of the use of sugar in the household of Simon de Montfort [1208-1265]). It was sold by the pound in the 13th century, and was obtainable in even such remote towns as Ross and Hereford. In an early account of Anglo-Venetian trade, *circa* 1319, there is an account of a shipment made at Venice for England of 10,000 pounds of sugar-candy.

The actual preparation of sweetmeats in England is mentioned by a variety of writers. Caxton, in the *The Game and Playe of the Cheese*, (1474) refers to the confectioners as 'they that make confeccions and confites and medecynes', and Bacon's *Naturall Historie* (1627) states: 'They have in Turkey and the East certain confections which they call serverts [Sherberts?] which are like to candied conserves, and are made of sugar and lemons'.

Sweetmeat Boxes

Left and right
Large Victorian silver-gilt Pyx: the back engraved with the 'Angus Dei' and floral motifs: fleurs-de-lys in a neo-Gothic cartouche, and the front (not shown) with The Crucifixion and sorrowing angels. With 'snap' fastener and five-lugged hinge and on cast and pierced suspensory loop. Engraved in the lid with The Sacred Monogram in Pugin's neo-Gothic script.
Makers: John Hardman & Co. Birmingham 1849.
Size: 3 inches in diameter by ½ an inch deep. (This article is discussed in the text).
By courtesy of Monseigneur R. J. Foster, the Rector of St. Mary's College, Oscott, Warwickshire.

The monumental *The Jewels and Plate of Queen Elizabeth I*, taken from the Inventory of 1574, edited by A. Jeffries Collins, 1955, includes an intriguing entry (page 584, item 1557): 'One Cvmfett box Sylver gylte Fasshyoned Lyke a Tortoyes with a Lyttle folding Sponne ther in poiz. [weight] vj oz. qyarter'. Mr. Collins states that Queen Elizabeth 'received a number of other comfit boxes for sweetmeats as New Year's gifts. They do not appear in this inventory, however, because they were classed as jewellery, not as plate, and were committed to the charge of the Gentlewomen of the Privy Chamber. Thus the 'littill box of gold to put in cumphetts, and a litill spone of golde', presented by Blanche Parry in 1578, and the 'Comfett box of mother of pearles gar. wth gold and sett wth small sparks of Rubies, received from Lord [Henry] Seymour in 1589, were entrusted respectively to Lady Howard of Effingham, later Countess of Nottingham, and Mistress Mary Radclyffe. The present box was also originally in the keeping of Lady Howard. It appears towards the end of both copies of the inventory of the jewellery for which she was responsible thus: 'A Comfitt Box of Siluer gilt Fashioned lyke a Tortes wth vij stones iij of them Christalles the ground painted with flowers, the iiij other stones being Conelians (sic) and a Lytle siluer Spoone, geven by Mr Arthur Frogmorton'. This 'little tortois box' with the other plate

still in the Upper Jewel-house at the Tower, fell into the hands of the Parliament in August 1649 . . .

As a result of Commonwealth sequestration, very few 'comfit or sweetmeat boxes' of true provenance remain extant: it is only possible, by study of the form of the box itself, its closely fitting lid, the 'drop-over' or 'snap' fastener, and, sometimes, a contemporary mention, to arrive at its probable use. Thus, the Exhibition of Royal and Historic Treasures held at 145 Piccadilly in 1939, contained (item 3, page 49, in the catalogue) 'One comfit box belonging to Lord Darnley with his initials 'H.S.' engraved on it'. The item was loaned to the Exhibition by the Earl of Galloway. It will be recalled that Henry Stuart, Lord Darnley (1545-1567) was the second husband of Mary, Queen of Scots, and the father of King James I of England. He was deeply involved in both political and personal intrigues, and died under highly suspicious circumstances.

The delightfully austere oval Sweetmeat Box illustrated was wrought in 1651, and, on reflection, is a surprising manifestation of Puritan indulgence: at a time when most sumptuous plate was frowned upon as 'frivolous luxury', the commission of, and execution by, a Commonwealth craftsman of such a beautiful article, is inexplicable. The silversmith obviously attempted to conform to the austerity of the times, as the receptacle is really nothing more than a hinged-lid box with a massive 'hinge-drop' fastening, and, with the exception of the pricked initials and date '1652' in a primitive floral device, there is no other embellishment. As the article is, however, fully hall-marked, there can be no question that it was clandestinely wrought: it was made with the full sanction of the Commonwealth authorities. The only other possible explanation might be that its intended function was disguised in some way—it might have been originally described as a 'bible-box', but this is highly conjectural, and very unlikely.

Commonwealth large oval elliptical sweetmeat box: of austerely plain form. The lid of the 'stepped' variety, that is, the top ellipse is slightly higher than the rim. With 'drop-over' fastening.
Maker: **A.F.** in shield, London 1651.
Size: 7½ inches by 5¾ inches by 2½ inches deep.
Weight: 17 ozs. 8 dwts.
Pricked on the lid with contemporary initials and the date '1652'.
Courtesy of the Worshipful Company of Goldsmiths.

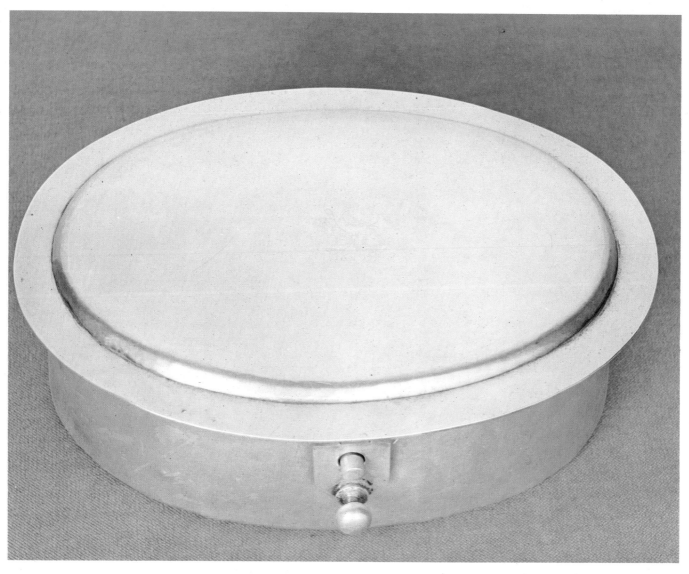

Oval Amatory Spiceboxes

As far as may be presently ascertained, this type of container has always been taken for granted as a receptacle for spices. The term somehow attached itself, though, except for the country of origin of the motifs, as will be shown, there is little provenance to link this object with spice.

The type is well-known: it is a little oval box with 'pinch-sides', that is, a device whereby, on pressing the sides, the slightly convex, tightly fitting lid is 'sprung' open, although there is no actual spring inside the lid. It is usually engraved on the top with a primitive 'Cherub' subject and some sort of motto either in Latin or French, and normally possesses only a maker's mark of the 1685-95 period.

Yet, on closer examination, there are some very interesting aspects which invite careful scrutiny. The first question to be investigated is that of the origin of the *genre*, that is, the source from which the style was taken or copied. Before this may be undertaken, however, it is essential to describe the type of engraving which may be encountered: the majority of such boxes illustrate single cherubs or 'amorini', usually against a background of landscape or architecture, and sometimes these figures bear 'love-arrows' or gaze on a 'heart upon a burning altar', or at a rosebush. All such boxes bear mottoes 'scratch-engraved' within 'motto-ribbons' at the top, usually in Latin, French, or, very occasionally, in English.

The essential clue to this enigmatic group lies in the 'emblems' engraved on the lids, for the term 'emblem' signifies 'a picture expressing a moral fable or allegory', and such subtle messages were very much admired throughout the 17th century. There was even a group of poets known as 'The Emblematists', and one of the most famous of these, though not necessarily the most profound, was the English writer, Francis Quarles (1592-1664). His work consisted of a series of paraphrases from Scripture, expressed in ornate and metaphorical language, followed by a passage from the Christian Fathers, and concluding with an epigram of four lines. This type of 'emblem' was defined as 'Sacred', but there were also 'Profane Emblems', which copied the work of Quarles and his contemporaries, but which introduced amatory subjects into the text.

The mottoes were very innocent (except perhaps to the recipient) and consisted of such messages as *To the most faithful*, or, *With you as my leader, I am not blind*, and, sometimes, where a burning heart is shown upon an altar, the message might be: *I shun, but I burn, (Arceo sed ardeo)*. These mottoes are mostly in French and Latin—English versions are rarer.

It is now possible to return to the question of the original *genre*, and the subject may perhaps best be tackled from an historical angle. It is well-known, for instance, that love emblems flourished throughout Holland in the 17th century, and the distinguished Jacob Cats (1577-1660) wrote his *Emblemata* in 1618. The great Flemish painter, and Master of Rubens, Otto Van Veen (otherwise known as 'Vaenius') engraved a series of 'Emblemata' known as *Amorum Emblemata*, which was published in Antwerp in 1615, and which was, in turn, based upon the renowned engravings by Crispin van de Passe the Elder (1565-1637) which were known as *Thronus Cupidinis*; this group of engravings was far more elaborate than the simply 'scratched' amorini appearing on the boxes, but the *genre* is thus established.

William III oval engraved lid spicebox: with five-lugged 'stand-away' hinge, and soldered on 'side-pieces', the pressing of which eased the tension on the lid for opening, and 'snap' catch inside box. The lid engraved with 'Emblemata Amatoria' motif depicting a cherub pointing arrows at an altar bearing a heart aflame, and the motto 'Vn sevl me blesse' —One alone injures me'—This motto and others of the type are discussed in the text.
Maker: **IG** Crowned, London *circa* 1695. (*vide* Jackson, page 142, line 17)
Size: 1¾ inches by 1¼ inches by ⅝ of an inch deep.

Much more to the point, however, both from a practical point of view, and because the 'Love Poems' as they are called, are printed in four languages: Latin, English, Italian and French, and illustrated by simpler engravings, is a little book entitled *Emblemata Amatoria*, or *Cupid's Adresse to the Ladies*; the poems were penned by Philip Ayres (1638-1712) the author of numerous books and pamphlets, who was active in the latter part of the 17th century, and the engravings were by an artist whose enigmatic cypher has been variously interpreted as that of Isaac Beckett of London, or Jan Van Vianen (circa 1660 died after 1719), who was known as an engraver of historical subjects.

The book was published in London in 1683, about the same time as the oval silver 'spiceboxes' appeared. It would have been too much to expect of History that the very mottoes and love poems which Ayres wrote in his charming little book should appear within the motto-ribbons on the boxes, but the gist is often very similar. Where, for instance, the engraving depicts a cherub plucking roses, the poem is headed 'The Difficult Adventure' and states:

> While wanton love in gathering Roses strayes
>> Blood from his hands, and from his eyes drop tears,
> Let him poor Lovers pitty, who tread wayes,
>> Of bloody prickles, where no Rose appears.

This verse, if simply paraphrased, would be 'No Rose without Thorns', which motto indeed appears on one of the oval boxes illustrated, and the subject, with a simplified architectural scene in the background, could be the very example used!

It has, then, to be borne firmly in mind, that the original engravings from which these 'emblems' are taken, are of Low Countries origin, although some specimens bear mottoes in French (which was then, as now, an international language) because this provenance might have yet another important bearing upon the design of the article. It has been noted that as opposed to purely English oval boxes, which were 'hand-raised' that is, beaten up from a single sheet of silver, these little boxes are often composed of three layers of metal: the concave base, an elliptical 'middle' and the convex lid, all subtly soldered together to constitute the whole, and frequently engraved around the ellipse with a band of that primitive 'debased laurel' motif which is such a feature of most oval boxes of the period. The motif itself, namely, the 'laurel' wreath running round the rim, has ancient Chinese origins, and is even found on mid-16th century Turkish Pottery of the Isnik region of Asia Minor, and was applied to the 'spiceboxes' in order to disguise the joint between the portions.

Yet another aspect, which has been noted after careful comparative study is that the majority of Dutch and Flemish boxes possess 'stand-away' hinges, that is, instead of the 'integral hinge' which is such a feature of the 18th century French boxes, where the hinge is completely hidden from view, the Netherlands specimens have wide flanges, or rims which stand away from the bezel of the box itself, thus permitting the lid to open much wider. The 'integral hinge' has been noted on jewelled book-covers, caskets and belt-buckles, as far back as Anglo-Saxon times, so it is nothing new, but it might be opportune to devote some space to a survey of 'the hinge through history' which might serve to throw a little further light on an obscure and studiously ignored aspect.

The Box Hinge

Most box-hinges noted, whether of ecclesiastical or secular function were until the beginning of the 18th century of the 'knuckle and lug' variety. That is, the lid would have the 'lug' or ears, and the base would have the 'knuckles', which then united the top and bottom of the box by means of the traverse 'pintle' or bolt. Thus, most hinges would have three, five or even seven knuckles and lugs, which for brevity's sake will henceforth be referred to as 'lugged'.

The first signs that the hinge had become an important feature of 'fastening' arrived with the ivory Diptychs (folding Altar-pieces composed as two leaves) of the late 13th-early 14th centuries, which have base-metal 'three-lugged' hinges cut into the ivory, and which, like their later descendants, the Netherlands boxes, 'stand-away' from the edge, to permit the plates to open fully, yet also allow them to close fairly tightly.

This 'knuckle and lug' feature is not confined to French and Flemish work, but may be observed on Italian, Spanish and German Diptychs, Triptychs (three-fold panels) and Caskets. This 'three-lugged' method of fastening was, of course, carried to the hinges of vessels, and tankards, ewers, and even the mounts of coconut cups, shells and mazers all possessed them.

Most hinges of the 17th century are of the 'stand-away' type, and possess three or five lugs, and, very often, this feature alone can reveal an important clue to the age of the article, even in the absence of any 'marks'. An interesting and curious example of the foreign 'stand-away' hinge is to be found in William Hone's *Table Book*, dated London 1827. This illustrates (pp. 527–29) an intriguing large heart shaped silver box with 'stand-away' three-lugged hinges at either side of the rims. The receptacle is engraved to simulate the human heart, and the story surrounding the article is macabre yet fascinating.

Lord Edward Bruce, son of Sir Edward, baron of Kinloss, was killed in a duel at Bergen-op-Zoom, a small Dutch town, not far from the Flemish border. The date was 1613. Tradition had maintained that Bruce's heart was sent home and interred in the old abbey church of Culross in Perthshire. Bruce had been challenged by Sir Edward Sackville on what appears to be a 'trumped-up' charge. In 1808, a search was made and a silver box containing the embalmed heart was found. After a careful sketch had been made (which Hone illustrates) the relic was reinterred.

Here, then, is an unimpeachable Netherlands specimen of the 'stand-away' type of hinge of early 17th century provenance, and when it is further recalled that the little oval 'spiceboxes' are enriched with 'amatory motifs' of early Dutch origin, and that, furthermore, they almost invariably possess three or five lugged 'stand-away' hinges this origin is thereby confirmed, although of course, the articles themselves were made in England.

The inference that because they are usually found in three subtly soldered sections does not preclude them from being purely English in origin. The clever English craftsmen, having already copied the enrichment and 'emblems' from Dutch and other foreign influences, would hardly hesitate to employ foreign methods, though the normal type of English box would have been 'hand-raised'. The larger oval snuffboxes with the same type of 'stand-away' hinge might thus also be originally of Netherlands influence.

The Eighteenth Century Hinge

The advent of the 18th century brought one important development: the hinge was gradually moved away from the rim of the container towards the centre. Thus, an oval silver-mounted cowrie-shell snuffbox would have a band of delicate diaper engraving at both the apex and the nadir of the box, that is, there would be a disguised hinge within the top band of the diaper engraving, probably of the five-lugged variety, and no hinge at all in the bottom design, but both motifs would be exactly matching. The engraved ornament, of course, would be quite symmetrical both top and bottom. Sometimes, when it was not possible to engrave top and bottom bands of embellishment on the lid, attention would be drawn away from the hinge by means of a grotesque mask engraved within a cartouche of foliate motifs, and, of course, in the case of the 'bright-cut' specimens, where the quality of the engraving was such that the brilliant facets distracted the eye completely, it might not even be considered necessary to disguise the hinge at all.

The Nineteenth Century Hinge

The 'integral hinge' so beloved of writers on snuffboxes, while a feature of French and German containers from the early 1730's, was quite well-known on other hinged articles—Dutch 'Marriage Caskets', Hispano-Moresque Caskets, Iberian Caskets, from the 15th to the mid-17th centuries—on any article, in fact, where fine workmanship was demanded. The traverse pin within the finely rolled hinged cylinder which was soldered to the very edge of the bezel eventually developed as an inexpensive type of hinge, and from the early 1820's, is found on almost all hinged lid receptacles. Sometimes, as in the work of the Birmingham craftsmen of the mid 1840's, the hinge was so successfully disguised that it may be deduced that a specialist hinge-maker might have spent days (at a time when labour was all too cheap) on one superlative article. It has been endeavoured, in this present work, to illustrate the virtuosity of the various schools of hinge-makers, as this minor art is so frequently taken for granted.

Counter Boxes

Another small, yet highly important silver box is the familiar 'Counter Box'. These little circular containers are well-known to all collectors of 17th century *bibelots*: they are usually about 1¼ inches high by 1½ inches in diameter, and when fully complete, contain between twenty and thirty-seven counters. The designs on these very thin 'coin-like' discs vary considerably; some have floral motifs of Dutch or Flemish influence, others bear the portraits of English Sovereigns, a very few have Biblical themes (scenes from the Gospels) there is even a

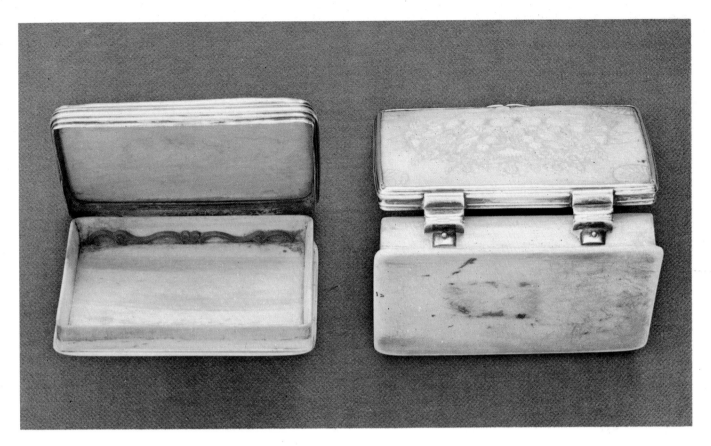

William III small shallow rectangular silver-mounted ivory snuffbox: with three-lugged 'stand-away' hinges. The yellowing ivory lid carved with 'Ceres and Cupid' motif and scallop shells in the corners. The hinges and the retaining clasp are of brass.
Unmarked *circa* 1695.
Size: 2¾ inches by 2⅛ inches by ¼ of an inch deep.

William III shallow rectangular silver-mounted ivory snuffbox: with three-lugged 'stand-away' hinges. The lid carved with a 'basket of fruit and flowers' motif, and scallop shells and a cherub in the corners and at the base. Simple shaped thumbpiece.
Unmarked, *circa* 1695.
Size: 3 inches by 2½ inches by ¼ of an inch deep.

full set of the 'Cries of London' from the period of Charles I, based on a 'broadside' of the period, and enumerating such delightful occupations as: 'Bandstringes for hankercher buttons; Buy my Hartichokes Mistris; Matt for a bed buy a Doore matt; Maribones Maides Maribones; I have Screens if yow desier to keep yˢ. Buty from yˢ. fire; Radishes or lettis tow bunches a peny'. The itinerant sellers are dressed in mid-17th century costume and are all of sombre disposition.

It would, in this connection, be quite wrong to plagiarise the work of the late Miss Helen Farquhar (1859-1953) whose superbly researched articles on counters appeared from time to time in *The Numismatic Chronicle*, but some of her researches coincide so exactly with aspects in this present work, that they must, for this reason, be included here.

Miss Farquhar, basing her theories on her own wise observations and on the earlier work of G. F. Hill of the British Museum, came to the conclusion that many of the superlatively engraved counters found within Charles I 'counter-boxes' were not, in fact, hand-engraved, as had been quite legitimately believed hitherto, but the work of the clever Dutch medallist Simon van de Passe (*circa* 1595-*circa* 1637), who had invented a method whereby a steel die was cut and wafer-thin discs of silver were struck with the motifs, thereby imitating engraving by hand. Grueber's *magnum opus: Medallic Illustrations of the History of Great Britain and Ireland*, published by the British Museum between 1906-11, in the notes referring to Plate XXXIV (where counters struck between 1625-1638 appear) states: 'These are stamped in imitation of engraving. They were used as markers or counters for reckoning and for play . . . The period over which the issue of these pieces ranges is from 1616 to 1638, the earlier date corresponding with that when Simon Passe commenced his portraits of various members of the Royal Family and others. When the present work comes to the analysis of 19th century ornament the connection with Miss Farquhar's discoveries will become apparent. It becomes necessary to examine their probable use. To pass them off as mere 'gaming counters' would be highly inviting (and possibly even partially correct) but there is much more to these little objects than a purely frivolous use.

Thomas Snelling's treatise *A view of the Origin, Nature and use of Jettons, or Counters*, printed in London, 1762, defines the term 'counter' literally, a disc which was used as a 'counting device' by an ignorant person unskilled in mathematical calculation. After citing various European terms for these 'counters'—he traces the word from the French verb 'jet(t)er', to cast or throw—Snelling enumerates the instances, made towards the close of the 15th century, of gifts of jettons, at public expense, to various dignitaries, in magnificent purses and silver boxes ornamented on the lids with the Arms of the Province or the City of Origin, and each example bore emblems, inscriptions and Royal Portraits. This practice is of course, yet another manifestation of the Biblical adage 'Unto every one that hath shall be given'—these counters were originally intended to serve the poor ignorant peasant, and became eventually a magnificent New Year's gift for the mighty . . .

The famous numismatist Francis Pierrepoint Barnard in his *The Casting Counter and the Counting Board* (this last was a device whereby the drudgery of counting by hand could be speeded up) cites many historical origins for counter boxes. In 1496 and 1540 a 'nest of counters' is mentioned: in 1583 'a case of lyon counters' (presumably because they had lions struck on their surfaces), and in 1628, 'a box and counters'. In a footnote, Barnard suggests that the box of van de Passe's counters exhibited at the New Gallery in 1889 as part of the Exhibition of the Royal House of Stuart, 'probably contained play-pieces'. This statement is of great service to the student, as it establishes, once and for all, the fact that where counters are in pierced and die-struck circular boxes (such as illustrated in this work) these were probably used by the nobility during gambling games, and where the box-lid has a die-struck portrait of either Charles I or Charles II, this was intended as a clandestine allusion to the Martyrdom of the House of Stuart.

It is interesting that whereas English counter-boxes are almost invariably completely circular, the Dutch and French examples tend to taper towards the base; it may be possible that several sizes of counters were in use on the continent, the smaller being placed at the bottom of the box, and the larger at the top. In passing, Barnard tells the amusing anecdote recounted by Ouville (*Les Contes aux Heures Perdues*, Volume II of the 1644-52 edition) that a bridegroom, who had tried in vain to sum up his expenses on his fingers, in desperation forgot all about the expectant bride, and, drawing his jettons from his pockets, set himself to cast his account with their aid . . .

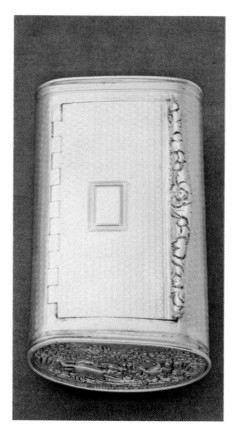

Much has been written elsewhere (vide *Investing in Silver*, pp. 104–5) about the fascinating little object, the patchbox, but recent researches have revealed further interesting material: The very earliest use of the 'patch' as a cosmetic aid was in classical Rome, and it was a general practice amongst women in the closing years of the Empire; men apparently also used patches to excite the curiosity of their ladies, for Henry Glapthorne (working between 1639–43) in his *Lady's Privilege*, 1640, says: 'If it be a lover's part you are to act, take a black spot or two. I can furnish you; 'twill make your face more amorous, and appear more gracious in your mistress' eyes'. Finally, in a volume issued in 1658 called *Wit Restored*, the following allusion to 'patching' appears:

> 'Her patches are of every cut,
>   For pimples or for scars;
> Here's all the wandering planet's signs,
>   And some of the fixed stars;
> Already gummed to make them stick,
>   They need no other sky.'

Patchboxes

George IV rectangular oval 'cushion-shaped' snuffbox: the lid, which has an 'integral-hinge', and the sides engine-turned with alternating bands of 'barleycorn' and 'wave' motifs, the sides with cast 'hunting' motifs. The thumbpiece is of the cast floral variety.
Maker: IJ, London 1828.
Size: 3½ inches by 2¼ inches by ¾ of an inch deep.
This maker is neither at Goldsmiths' Hall nor in Jackson.

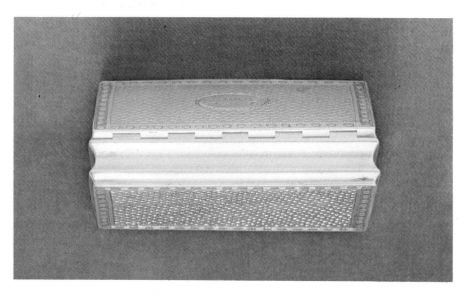

Tenon and mortise hinge of the box shown on page 63

The 'death-knell' of the practice appears to have come during the mid-18th century: a writer in *The World* of 1754, speaks of the patch increasing in size as to almost overwhelm the face ...

Some patchboxes are quite large, and during the 17th and early 18th centuries only lift-off lids have been noted, none hinged. One delightfully engraved English example, though embellished with a Dutch inspired 'tulip motif', appears within these pages; by virtue of the maker's mark and the primitiveness of the engraving, its date may be tentatively set as of *circa* 1660. Other patchboxes were very small, no more than ¾ of an inch in diameter and quite shallow, but of heavy gauge metal and ranging in date between 1680 and 1720. While it is possible that foreign specimens infiltrated into England, most of the examples noted have been of purely English provenance: some have contemporarily engraved cyphers or initials and, occasionally, a date roughly 'scratched' on the base; others have unimpeachable English makers' marks struck several times, both on the base and inside the lid.

Skippet Boxes & Sealing Wax

Curiously enough, while many thousands of steel, bronze and silver dies for seal matrices, that is, the finally cast seal, remain extant, little is known about the boxes which eventually preserved the actual wax impressions (originally very brittle) and then traditionally encased them for ceremonial reasons in metal 'skippets' or boxes. Early references to 'skippet boxes' are scant; primarily, the term of which several variations are known, chiefly 'skibbet', refers to a small box or compartment in a chest, used for the preservation of documents or seals. The Caxton version of Guillaume de Guilleville's poem *The Pylgremage of the Sowle* (written about 1330, and printed *circa* 1483) states: 'In her hond she brought a Skypet, and she took forth the Charter'.

That tireless researcher, Edward Alfred Jones, in a short article in *Apollo*

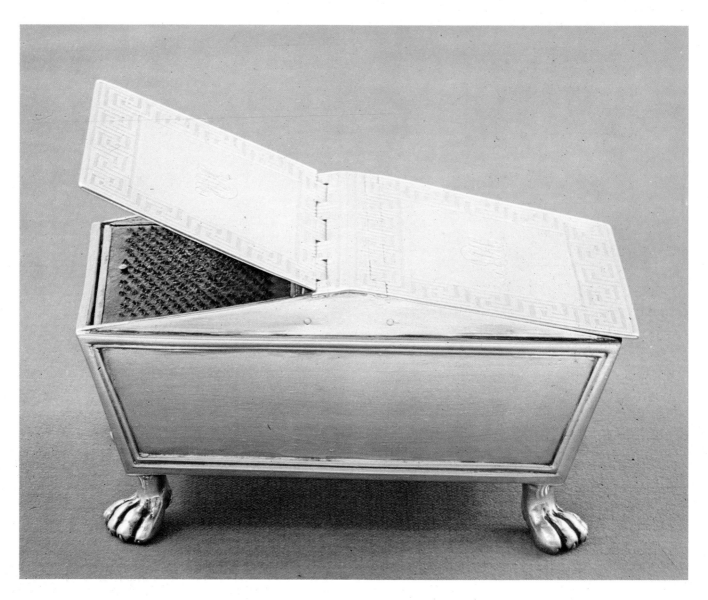

Magazine of December, 1934, illustrated a superbly engraved oval elliptical Skippet Box, still with the plaited tassel which normally runs through the seal (and provision for which is made in the base of the box by means of a slit at either end) attached. This oval silver box is engraved with the Arms of the University of Cambridge and the Coat-of-Arms of the Duke of Albermarle, quartering Monck, Plantagenet, Grey and Talbot within the Garter. 'From the fact that the second Duke was Chancellor of the University from 1682 until his death in 1688' says Jones, 'it is assumed that the box was provided for him'. A local antiquarian researcher, A. S. F. Gow, Esq., Fellow of Trinity College, discovered in the accounts for the making of the box, the name of a local Cambridge goldsmith, one Samuel Urlin, an apprentice (1647–1654) of the London goldsmith, Robert Welstead. Some five years after his admission as a Freeman of the Goldsmiths' Company, Urlin settled in Cambridge and worked there until his death in 1698, when he was succeeded by his son, Samuel.

Another University Sealbox had been supplied and probably made by another Cambridge goldsmith, John Disbrow, who had been apprenticed to the London goldsmith, John Ward from 1661 to 1668, and this particular specimen was made for the Duke of Monmouth in 1674.

The two Skippet boxes illustrated in this work bear the mid-18th century Coats-of-Arms of the University of Oxford, and one contains a mediaeval seal of the Chancellor of the University. It has not been possible to trace the identity of the maker whose maker's mark alone appears on both specimens: **RG** in Old English script. There is nothing in the Plate Register at Goldsmiths' Hall to hint at the possible identity of this silversmith, whose mark, on various other small articles, has been noted up to *circa* 1760. It does not appear to be Robert Garrard's early mark.

Even less is known of the materials which constituted 'sealing wax', not the modern 'shellac' variety, but the mediaeval and early 16th century types. Only

Above
George III table spice-box cum nutmeg grater: formed as rectangular sarcophagus with tapering sides and sloping lids, which have superbly fitted 'integral-hinges'. On four 'claw' feet, the lids engraved with 'Greek Key' motifs and contemporary monograms. The steel graters set in brass frames, and hinged to permit access to the grated nutmeg.
Maker: John Edwards, London 1805.
Size: 5 inches by 2½ inches by 2½ inches deep.

Right
Pair George II skippet or seal boxes: of oval elliptical form, the lids engraved with typical mid-Georgian scrolling cartouches in which are the Arms of Oxford University. The seal illustrated is that of a mediaeval Chancellor of the University. There are slits at the top and bottom of the boxes to permit the tassels or seal-strings to protrude.
Maker: **RC** in Gothic characters, London *circa* 1740. This maker is not in the Register at Goldsmiths' Hall, and the box is discussed in the text.
Size: 3 inches by 2¼ inches by ½ an inch deep.

John Beckmann, Professor of Economy at the University of Göttingen in Sweden, whose fascinating *History of Inventions, Discoveries and Origins*, published originally in German, *circa* 1780–1805, examined the substance thoroughly, and traced the origins from Egyptian Dynastic times, to the Romans, and the Byzantine emperors. It would appear that coloured sealing wax was already in use in 1524, when Charles V granted a Dr. Stockamar of Nuremberg the privilege of using blue wax in seals. The oldest mention of sealing wax which Beckmann had noted in printed books was the work of Garcia ab Orto, *circa* 1563, and the oldest printed recipe for making sealing wax appeared in a work by Samuel Zimmerman, citizen of Augsburg, printed in 1579; the following is an abstract:

'To make hard sealing-wax, called Spanish wax, with which if letters be sealed they cannot be opened without breaking the seal:—take beautiful clear resin, the whitest you can procure, and melt it over a slow coal fire. When it is properly melted, take it from the fire, and for every pound of resin add two ounces of vermillion, pounded very fine, stirring it about. Then let the whole cool, or pour it into cold water. Thus you will have beautiful red sealing wax. If you are desirous of having black wax, add lamp-black to it. With smalt (finely pulverised glass of azure pigmentation) you may make it blue, with white lead white, and with orpiment (yellow arsenic) yellow. If, instead of resin, you melt purified turpentine in a glass vessel, and give it any colour you choose, you will have a harder kind of sealing-wax, and not so brittle as the former'.

Finally, the imposing circular silver-gilt Seal-case by John Bridge of London, 1826, with the embossed Royal Coat-of-Arms of George IV on the lid was probably intended to accommodate an Ambassadorial Seal, but all provenance has been lost. Certainly, it is an impressive container worthy of His Britannic Majesty's Ambassador to any nation in the world!

Right
Victorian 'writing etui': comprising inkpot, sealing-wax holder, taper-holder, sandbox, and stampbox, all set within rectangular box of heavy gauge silver. When closed, this receptacle reveals no clue to its purpose. Maker: Thomas Johnson, London, 1869. Size: 4 inches by 2½ inches by 1 inch deep. This maker is entered in the Register at Goldsmiths' Hall, London, as a 'smallworker' and registered his mark on the 15th of October 1869. His workshop was at 10 Dyer's Buildings, Holborn, and his mark was **TJ** in an oval punch. He made novelty articles, chiefly small, but finely conceived boxes.

George III circular 'Bougie-box': with reeded rims top and bottom and 'fold-in' buckle-shaped handle, and sliding half-crescent cover on domical lid. With 'stand-away' five-lugged hinge, and engraved with contemporary monogram.
Makers: Phipps and Robinson, London, 1784-5 (marked with King's Head Incuse). Size: 2 inches in diameter by 1¼ inches deep.

Below
George IV large circular silver-gilt sealbox: with oakleaf motif border and 'stand-away' hinge, and embossed and chased with the Royal Coat-of-Arms of George IV embracing the Order of the Garter and with the 'George' pendant below:
Maker: John Bridge, London, 1826. Size: 6 inches in diameter by 1⅜ inches deep.

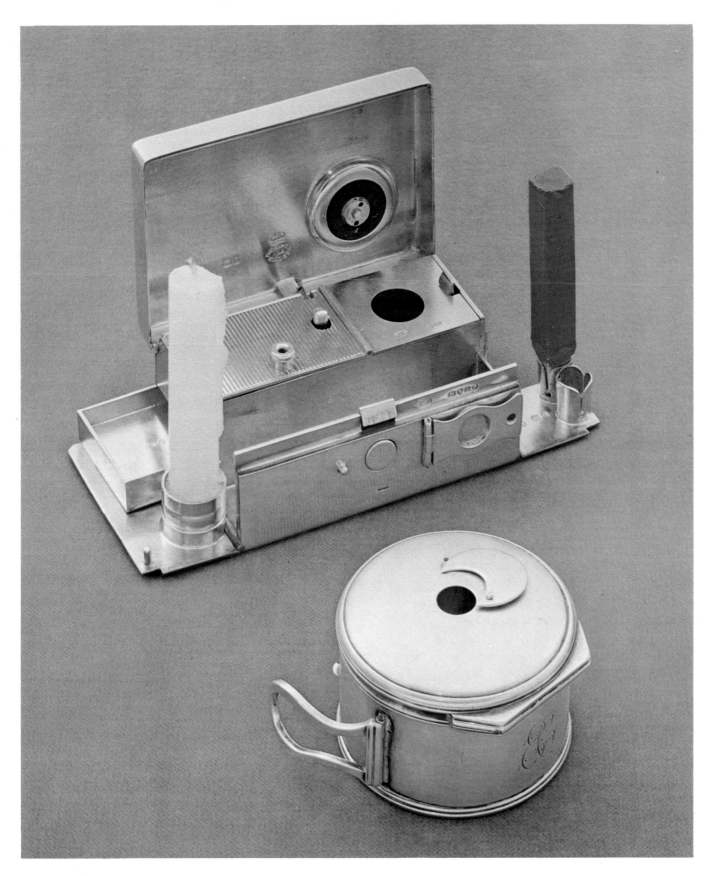

Dental
Boxes

It is always very difficult to be dogmatic about the original use of an article many generations after the death of the people who invented it. Many such 'inventions' of which, no doubt, their owners were justly proud, are now nothing more than an irritatipg enigma to present-day researchers. Yet it has to be continually borne in mind that all the curious, unusual and useful boxes illustrated within these covers, were once owned and cherished by normal, respectable people. When, in the course of time, they bequeathed their treasures to their heirs, these might have been stolen, mistreated, or, finally and ignominiously sent to the sale-room by indifferent beneficiaries, and their real

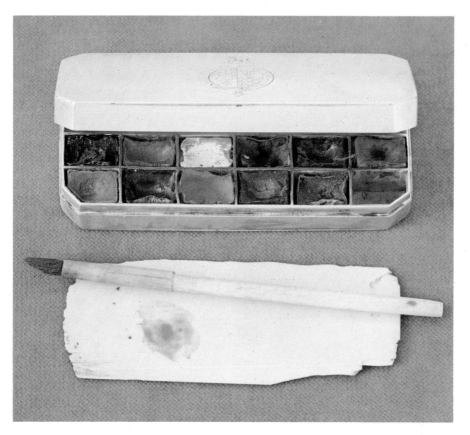

George III rectangular cut-corner artist's water-colouring box: with twelve colour compartments containing contemporary pigments. Also in the box are an ivory palette and an ivory handled paint-brush.
Unmarked *circa* 1770.
Size: 3½ inches by 1½ inches by ½ an inch deep.
The otherwise plain lid engraved with the Arms of the Gresley Family of Derbyshire. The owner of the box, Nigel Bowyer Gresley succeeded to the barony (created in 1611) in 1787.
This box was probably made to commission, but its fine lines point to a metropolitan origin rather than a local silversmith's work. Paintboxes, even in base metal, are uncommon but two examples have been noted, although, of course, other examples must exist: One, in metal, is in the Victoria and Albert Museum. This originally belonged to the famous English Miniaturist George Engleheart (1750-1829). The other is in the Royal Academy, and was given by the Duchess of Kent to her daughter Queen Victoria in 1837. This box, in a fitted rosewood case inlaid with tortoise-shell and ivory and with brass fittings, contains twenty-six syringes for oil paints, which device was the first of its kind. The box also contains a silver artist's ruler by Charles Rawlings, London 1827.

function temporarily lost to posterity.

Thus, who is to say, for instance, that the delightfully bright-cut rectangular containers here described as 'toothpick cases', are, in fact, of dental origin? 'Perhaps', some sceptical reader might retort, 'they were originally patchboxes?' Perhaps they were: it is possible that the silversmiths of the late 18th–early 19th centuries had finally arrived at the conclusion (not yet amounting to 'all-out mass-production') that one type of article might, if fitted out individually, have several different uses. The fact remains that most of the elliptical and rectangular cut-corner shallow boxes, lined with fading red velvet, which were intended as patchboxes, have tiny mirrors set within their lids, in much the same way as the modern 'ladies powder compacts' have in theirs. On reflection, a fully, or even partially filled patchbox of this type has never been noted, presumably because the patches were fragile and brittle, and, in any case, were probably used up long ago by their avid possessors. Very similar boxes, however, also with red velvet linings, but without mirrors, have been noted which contained several ivory toothpicks (and, occasionally, an ivory bodkin needle) still reposing inside them.

Strangely, very few 18th and 19th century toothpicks in precious metals appear to have survived in English boxes, although French and sometimes

Victorian 'cushion-shaped' nutmeg grater: of rectangular form and with 'blued steel' grater. The spice-compartment on the side with hinged lid, and the lid of the grater engraved to simulate smaller lid at other side, in order to provide 'continuity of design'. The reeded base has a finely concealed 'integral hinge' and the lids have scrolling thumbpieces. Engraved with contemporary monogram.
Makers: Charles Wallington and Shirley Deakin, Birmingham, 1863.
Marked in lid, inside base, and with lion passant on side.
Size: 4¾ inches by 1¼ inches by 1 inch deep.

Swiss specimens are occasionally encountered; the toothpick, apart from many mentions in classical literature, particularly Greek and Roman, was well-known to the Court of The Virgin Queen, and fascinating accounts of this specialised 'toilet accessory' appear in the aforementioned *Inventory of the Jewels and Plate of Queen Elizabeth I*, for instance, 'Item foure Touthe pickes of golde gevon by Mrs Snowe at new yers tide Anno predicto poiz all iiij d.wait. dim'. As Mr. Collins' footnote could hardly be improved upon, it is here given in full (apart from a few parenthetical genealogical references): 'Mistress Snowe seems to have been a widow, a Gentlewoman of the Privy Chamber who died in 1587. Rarely did she fail to offer a New Year's gift. In 1577 she produced 'vj Tothe pickes of golde and vj smale Clothes to wype Teeth wrought wᵗʰ blacke silke', (to replace the tooth-cleaning appliances given the previous year) and in 1574 she had given six toothpicks, one of which was lost by the Queen'. It has been said that the Queen suffered from defective teeth (F. Chamberlin, *Private Character of Elizabeth.* pp. 86–7, etc). Earlier in the Inventory (No. 1368) mention is made of a 'Touthe picke and Eare picke of like siluer guilt' which had been made for Queen Mary, but which had disappeared.

Also illustrated within this section is a charming little elliptical box of undoubted dental provenance: quite apart from its unusual design—it has an inner lid, hinged about one inch from the end of the ellipse, and with a steel 'snap' fastener at the other, the lid and base lined in green morocco leather—it still contains a set of 'scaling' instruments, one of which is a file, to cleanse between the upper front teeth, and the other a 'scaler' to remove tartar from the enamel, with further green morocco leather 'separators' between the instruments and a very clear mirror set in the lid. Careful scrutiny of the hall-marks struck on an elliptical cartouche on the red morocco leather lid has determined that the place of origin is Sheffield (quite normal as the instruments are of finely wrought steel) and the date 1825. The maker's mark, for some reason, has been deliberately obliterated. There is a band of beautiful bright-cut ornament around the top of the lid, and the whole receptacle is of delicate yet purposeful appearance. Presumably, the mirror in the lid had something to do with dental practice; it is even possible that it was used by the practitioner as a form of primitive dental mirror, but this is pure conjecture.

In early dental references two commentators stand out: *Paulus Aegineta*, a celebrated Greek surgeon of between the 4th and 7th centuries AD, who *inter alia* mentions a small raspatory (file) used for removing tartar from the teeth and adds 'The scaly concretions which adhere to teeth we may remove with the scoop of a specillum, or with a scaler or a file', and the earlier court physician to

Filigree as an ornamental medium has very early origins. Riisøen and Bøe's history of filigree in Norwegian ownership, *Om filigran*, published by the Oslo University Press in 1959 (which has a bi-lingual chapter in English) states that filigree work traces its ancestry back to Egyptian gold jewellery and was popular as a medium for both ecclesiastical plate and other vessels of Spanish and German origins from the Renaissance. The word 'filigree' appeared for the first time in French and English dictionaries *circa* 1650, and Sweden possessed an entire group of filigree masters, whose products were sent as gifts to the Emperors of Russia.

English 18th and 19th century specimens are very seldom marked for two reasons: the first that there is hardly any space upon which to strike a mark without damaging the delicate wirework, and the second, that the Act of 1758, which compelled silversmiths to obtain a licence for the manufacture of articles over 5 pennyweights in weight, exempted filigree work, providing they did not exceed the prescribed weight. As it is hardly likely that this filigree toothpick case weighed less than 5 dwts, even without its inner lining, some anomalies in marking must have existed. Birmingham as well as London, had filigree workers: one, John Smith, of 14 Newhall Street, is mentioned in the 1774 issue of Swinney's *Birmingham Directory*, and 'M. Kettle' of Suffolk Street, is in Wrightson and Webb's *The Directory of Birmingham* 1841, as a 'filigree button-maker'.

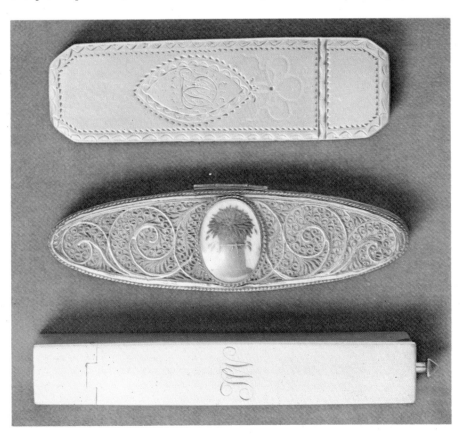

the emperor Claudius, *Scribonius Largus* (A.D. 47) mentions an excavator for similar purposes.

The toothbrush, as a substitute for the toothpick, appears to have developed during the second half of the 17th century. The very earliest toothbrushes were nothing more than a bundle of semi-abrasive animal hairs such as hog bristles set in a primitive tubular handle, and late 18th century specimens have been noted where a piece of ivory has been fashioned into a 'handle-like' instrument with a circular indented pad at one end, into which, presumably, the hairs were inserted (by the time the brushes were noted, nothing remained of the bristles).

The ingenuity of the European silversmith in creating new implements to the commission of his customers is legendary: towards the end of the 18th century, in both England and France, a new type of toothbrush appeared: this was, again, a simple silver shaped handle, but it had a rectangular frame at one end, into which a 'brush-pad' already wired with segmented bristles could be placed, and removed for easy cleaning. The type is well-known, and Napoleon had one in his elaborate travelling necessaire. Specimens are illustrated here, and the 'brush-pad' of one such fine toothbrush has been deliberately removed to show its form. Toothbrushes, once in existence, required further containers, in much the same manner as the 20th century plastic toothbrush container protects it from dirt and permits the bristles to dry out after use; a specimen of this type of silver box is also illustrated.

Finally, what of the dentifrice powders used by these early hygienists? Most of the early 19th century 'toothbrush kits' (a fine specimen of which, in its contemporary red morocco case appears here) had, in addition to the toothbrushes and tongue-scrapers (necessary items in an imbibing society) a little rectangular box with double hinges, disguised at the central hinge with a hint of fine bright-cutting. This was for a slightly abrasive tooth-powder. The 'toothbrushing enthusiast' of the mid-17th century, however, was less lucky than his later counterpart. Here, taken from Brooke's *A Queen's Delight* (London, 1660), is a recipe for 'MR. FERENE OF THE NEW EXCHANGE, PERFUMER TO THE QUEEN, HIS RARE DENTIFRICE, SO MUCH APPROVED AT COURT':

'First take eight ounces of Irios [sic] roots, also four ounces of Pomistone [a highly abrasive mineral more usually employed in erasing ink from parchments], and eight ounces of Cutel bone [the shell of the cuttle-fish, yet another abrasive, put in, perhaps to mystify the credulous, as the shell was rarely available], also eight ounces of mother of pearle, and eight ounces of Corral, and a

Above
George III shaped nutmeg grater: formed as 'snail', the lid and base, as well as the sides with 'corrugated concentric' enrichment, and projecting thumbpiece.
Maker: Matthew Linwood **v**, Birmingham 1804.
Size: 1¼ inches by 1 inch by ¾ of an inch deep.

George III oval elliptical nutmeg grater: with 'stand-away' hinge and finely bright-cut with foliate motifs on a 'threaded' ground. The base with fine 'integral-hinge'.
Makers: Peter and Ann Bateman, London 1795.
Size: 1¾ inches by 1⅛ inches.

George IV oval elliptical 'Dental Instruments' case: containing scaling instruments of steel. Lined with green morocco on the inner lid and red morocco on the outer. Set in the centre of lid with oval plaque bearing hallmarks and with mirror inside the lid. The rim delicately bright-cut with 'wriggle-motifs'. The top of the inner lid hinged and with 'snap' fastener. It is probable that toothpicks could be accommodated on the top surface of this inner lid.
Maker: No maker's Mark, Sheffield 1825.
Size: 4 inches by 1½ inches by ¼ of an inch deep.
This article is mentioned in the text.

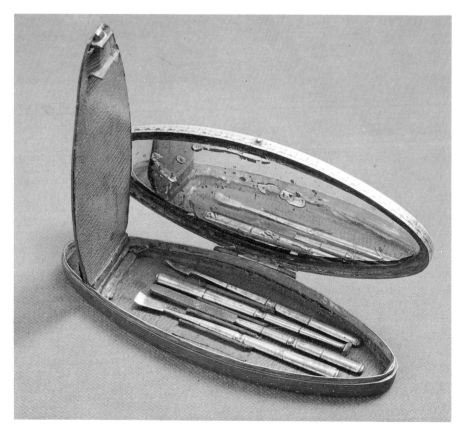

George III cylindrical nutmeg grater: with reeded bands on the body and near the rim, and gadrooned rim on top of the blued steel grater. With contemporary crest.

Maker: Matthew Boulton, Birmingham 1795. Small articles from Boulton's factory, especially at this date, are uncommon.

By courtesy of the Birmingham Assay Office.

Nutmeg graters have been discussed at length in *Investing in Silver* (pages 117–118) and will not be dealt with here, beyond the bare outline: they originated *circa* 1690, when they were made as silver-mounted cowrie-shells or tubular containers with silver tubular graters, and partially marked or totally unmarked. They did not develop in any great variety until the mid-18th century, and from the third quarter of the 18th to the second decade of the 19th centuries, a vast variety of different shapes were produced, mostly with blued steel graters, and fully marked. For further details, Mrs. Elizabeth B. Miles's *The English Silver Pocket Nutmeg Grater* (privately printed Cleveland, Ohio, USA, 1966) should be consulted.

Toilet Boxes

George III 'toothpowder box-cum toothbrush: of very uncommon type. The shaped stubby handle contains both a shallow powder-box, with its own hinged lid (of the three-lugged variety) and a toothbrush pad. The whole slides into the outer cover, and is completely disguised, appearing to be an ordinary rectangular box. The cover can be reversed to serve as handle.

Maker: Thomas Willmore, Birmingham *circa* 1790. (no date-letter)

Size: 3 inches by ½ an inch by ¼ of an inch deep.

pound of brown sugar candy and a pound of brick if you desire to make them red, but he did oftener make them white, and then instead of the brick did take a pound of fine Albablaster [sic]; after all this being thoroughly beaten, and sifted through a fine sieve, the powder is then ready prepared to make up in a paste, which must be done as follows:

TO MAKE THE SAID POWDER INTO PASTE

Take a little Gum Dragand [tragacanth] and lay it in steep twelve hours, in Orange water or Damask rose-water, and when it is dissolved, take the sweet gum, and grind it on a marble-stone with the aforesaid powder, and mixing some crumbs of whitebread, it will come into a paste, the which you may make dentifrices, of what shape or fashion you please, but long rolls is the most commodious for your use'.

Although later recipes were a trifle more merciful to the delicate tooth-enamel, and consisted mostly of chalk, camphor and borax, it is small wonder that only very few people of the 17th and 18th centuries had healthy teeth. Might it be too much to presume that the unsophisticated country lads and lasses died with the teeth with which they had been born, and that the cultured 'men about town' who followed fashion so devotedly, were left toothless; in fact, the higher the rank, the ranker the mouth?

It will probably have been noticed that certain celebrated types of boxes have been entirely omitted from this present evaluation of English Silver Boxes, and the famous 'shell-shaped' Spicebox of the Elizabethan era, is a good example of this omission. It is felt that such well-known articles have already received sufficient attention both from the antiques writers and the collecting public, and that concentration on lesser known types is the more valuable, in the long run. Thus, although only two specimens of the 'toilet box' variety are illustrated, no attempt has been made to include items from the well-beloved 'toilet services' of which the famous 'Lennoxlove Service' was only one outstanding example. The 'toilet box' is of interest here only because it is a type of contemporary container, whose function has been nebulous for many years, although vague hints about its contents have appeared in various articles.

Only two pre-Restoration Toilet Boxes have been noted: the first appears, yet once again, in *Queen Elizabeth's Inventory* as No. 1363: 'Item oone lie potte of siluer and guilt with a purslane hedde in the fore part thereof with a Couer

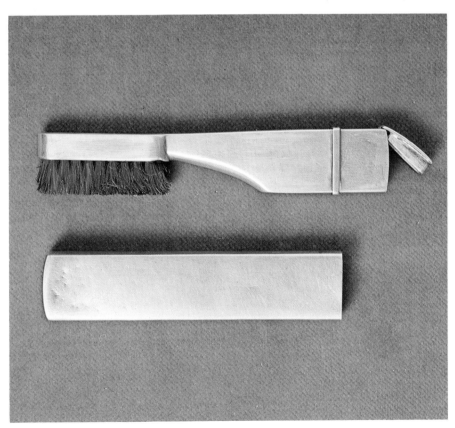

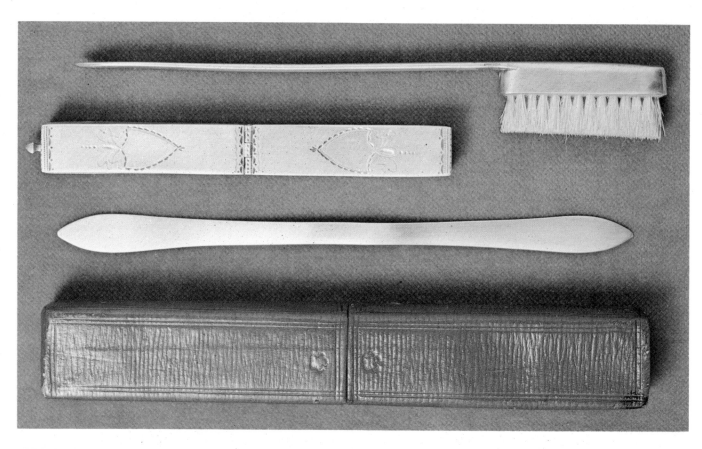

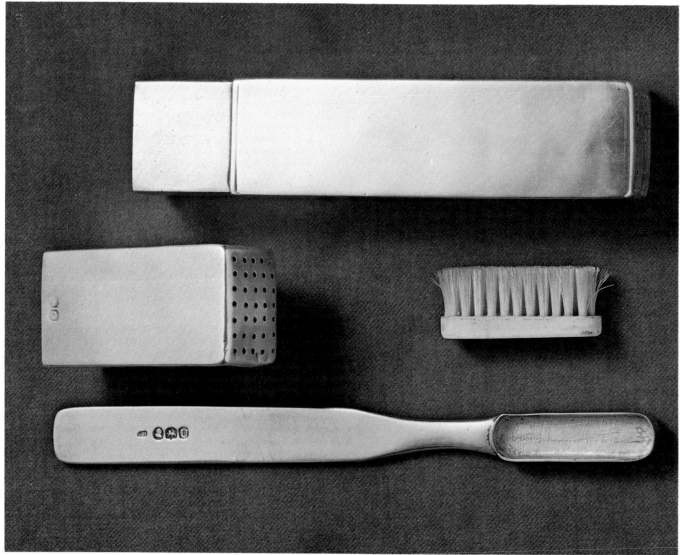

Upper left
George III 'Tooth Etui': comprising tooth-brush, with removable ivory brush-pad and plain tapering handle, double-ended tongue-scraper, and toothpowder box with double compartments hinged in centre with three-lugged 'integral-hinge' and with a diamond-shaped 'lifting-handle' on base. The lids bright-cut with 'shield and festoon' motifs In fitted red morocco contemporary case.
Maker: Joseph Taylor, Birmingham 1795.
Size: tooth-brush and tongue-scraper 4½ inches, toothpowder box 4 inches by ½ an inch by ¼ of an inch deep, case 6 inches by 1⅜ inches.

Lower left
George III silver-gilt toothbrush: of superb quality, the tapering rectangular handle terminating in 'pad-container', and with removable brush-pad. The bristles are bound in ivory with wire.
Maker: John Douglas, London 1815.
Size: 6 inches by ½ an inch.
John Douglas is in the Register at Goldsmiths' Hall, he entered his mark in 1813 and worked at 52 Red Lion Street, Clerkenwell.
This article is mentioned in the text.

George IV rectangular toothbrush case: of plain form and with removable lid. Pierced at one end for ventilation.
Maker: Archibald Douglas, London 1829.
Size: 7 inches by 1⅜ inches.
This article is mentioned in the text.
Archibald Douglas is in the Register at Goldsmiths' Hall; he worked with John (probably his father) at 52 Red Lion Street, when their mark was **ID/AD** in a square punch, but for himself at 15 West Street (the district is not given). Mark entered 1823.

[cover] standing in the backe thereof with a Coure having a round pece wherein is a Christall in place of a glasse enamelid vnder it with a shutting before the same poiz xxxv oz. iij quarters dim'. Once again, the footnote is highly enlightening: 'A "lye-pot" was an ornamental vessel to hold lye (alkalized water, usually a solution of potash) for use as a hair-wash'. the term, incidentally, is noted as far back as *circa* 1000. This 'lye-pot' is another form of toilet container which is not normally mentioned, and the 'Inventory' cites two other specimens, one of which was made for Queen Mary.

The second mention appears in the catalogue of the famous 'Magniac Collection sale, held at Christie's in July, 1892, and appears as No. 344 in the catalogue: 'A circular Flat-shaped Toilet Box and Cover, of silver-gilt engraved with band of Tudor Rose and other flowers, foliage and trellis ornament, London Hall-mark, 1589. 1¼ inches high'. Magniac was one of the most eminent collectors of *objets de vertu* of his day, and there is no reason to doubt his ascription.

What is interesting, and entirely absorbing is the enigma of what was placed within the perforated lidded toilet boxes (the present specimen is a late example): a superlative oval example by David Willaume, dated London 1720 was sold in a London saleroom in 1964, which possessed, in addition to the sturdy gauge box (the weight was 9 ozs. 8 dwts) a charmingly pierced rising-domed lid enriched with scroll motifs. Perhaps the answer lies in the fact that Willaume was a Huguenot craftsman and was thus influenced by some French custom—possibly a washing cloth was placed within the box and the perforated lid permitted it to air—it is hardly likely that such a large container would be used to contain perfume or soap (which, in any case, had its own spherical 'box'), similarly, the English silversmith who fashioned the opulent rectangular box with florally pierced centre panel, also made a complete 'Toilet Service' (this item is but one piece from it) in which there were other receptacles for toothbrushes, etc.

Medical Boxes

Perhaps one of the most fascinating of all the boxes illustrated within this group is the wholly delightful 'medicine box', which so greatly resembles a 17th century octagonal watch, complete with a delicately engraved florally enriched 'dial' and 'scratched' Roman numerals from I to XII. There is a typical five-lugged hinged octagonal lid, and the device is repeated on the back, with the exception that there are no 'works' inside the case. The box was originally made to contain powdered potions, and the user would set the 'hands' to the time of the next dosage. The 'acorn-shaped' baluster finial and the 'snap' type fastener are typically English in style.

Another rare receptacle is illustrated: a 'Caul Case'. Without going into intimate details of natal coincidence, it occasionally occurs that a baby is born with a 'caul' or remnant of membrane enveloping the head at birth; for some unknown reason, widespread superstitions became associated with the 'caul', and the most famed of all the fallacies connected with this is the belief that the owner of a caul would be preserved from drowning. An advertisement appearing in *The Times* as late as 1813 stated: 'To persons going to sea. A child's caul in a perfect state, to be sold cheap. Apply at 5 Duke Street, Manchester Square, where it may be seen'. This present 'caul-case' is heart-shaped and bears the owner's name and date of birth.

Below
George III silver-gilt rectangular toilet box: fully engine-turned with 'barleycorn' motif and with cast 'egg and dart' rim. The sides enriched with applique 'basketwork' motif, the lid embellished with scrolling acanthus and shell foliage. The centrally placed pierced panel finely conceived. With 'integral hinge.'
Maker: William Purse, London, 1815.
Size: 7 inches by 2¼ inches by 1⅜ inches deep.

Lancet or Phlebotomy Cases

The surgical practice of 'bleeding' or Phlebotomy, has very ancient origins indeed, and, quite often, was done with no thought of its therapeutic value. It is recorded, for instance, that there were 'four bleedings per annum' in the Cistercian abbey of Pipewell in Northamptonshire, and that in some monasteries the brethren were bled five times a year: in September, before Advent, before Lent, after Easter, and at Pentecost, which 'bleeding lasted three days'. This last practice was obviously connected with 'mortification of the flesh' and, as such, has no place here, but it is of interest, nevertheless.

In his *Early History of Surgery*, W. J. Bishop mentions that primitive peoples practiced various methods of 'bleeding' without any training in surgery, and enumerates three methods used by them today which almost exactly emulate mediaeval surgical practice. Of these—venesection—the direct opening of a vein, is widely popular. As early as 1380–1400, a Latin poem translated by Furnivall on 'The Manners and Meals in the Olden Time', and printed in the famous *Babees Book*, states:

'Phlebotomy clears the eyes, purifies
The minds & the brain, makes the marrows warm'

The great Milanese surgeon Lanfranc, whose standard work *Chirurgia Magna et Parva* was first printed *circa* 1490 gave surgeons a guide to phlebotomy: 'Indications for blood letting: a vein in the forehead is cut against headache and frenzy. A Blood-letting on the temples is good against Megrim [the mediaeval term for the modern 'migraine']. Give the patient a slice of bread and wine before the operation. Blood letting shall be used if a man eats and drinks too much, in cases of gout'.

A most interesting account of mid-17th century phlebotomy appears in Gladys Scott Thomson's *Life in a Noble Household* 1641–1700, which is a domestic history of the First Duke of Bedford, William Russell. The book itself is entirely fascinating, and the contemporary material contained therein of the utmost absorption. In the chapter headed 'In Sickness and in Death' (chapter XVI) the author cites two particular instances involving phlebotomy. The Earl Russell, then in his last years, took regular lettings of blood ('the health precautions' explains the author, 'customary at the time'). Furthermore, mention is made of Sir Edmund King, (who, as Dr. King, was a Court Physician) who was summoned to Whitehall when Charles II showed symptoms of what proved to be his last illness. While Dr. King was in the room, Charles fell down in a fit, whereupon King immediately bled him and the royal patient recovered consciousness. The other physicians, coming in, exclaimed that Dr. King had undoubtedly saved His Majesty's life, and the Privy Council, hearing of this, recommended a gratuity of a thousand pounds. It was never paid, for before the warrant could be signed, Charles was dead . . .' Further details of domestic 'bleeding' appear in the account-books of the family, and on various occasions, the surgeon charged 2 shillings and 6 pence for 'opening a vein'.

The practice of phlebotomy, as can be discerned, went on well into the Victorian era, as many of the finely wrought lancet cases stem from this period; most still have sets of razor-sharp lancets inside them, and some are most delicately enriched in the contemporary style of engraving.

Surgical Instrument Cases

Charles II rectangular shagreen covered instrument case: with silver 'stand-away' mounted hinges engraved with 'debased laurel' and floral motifs, and engraved on the pierced clasp with a 'sunflower' motif. The lid opening by means of a 'pushpiece' button. The interior lined with leather.
Unmarked, *circa* 1680.
Size: 6 inches by 2½ inches by 1½ inches deep.
'Shagreen' was made from untanned leather; it had a rough granular surface, and was prepared from the hide of the horse, ass, or sharks or seals. It was frequently dyed green. but naturally coloured specimens have been observed.

A letter which appeared in the correspondence columns of *Country Life* magazine on December 30th, 1954 under the heading 'Surgical Bygones' is of particular interest to the present survey for two reasons: one, that the photograph accompanying the letter illustrated a shagreen instrument case almost exactly duplicating the specimen here shown, and, two, that all the instruments were still intact, and, moreover, one was hall-marked for 1672. Thus a form of provenance is established between the two items, for very few complete surgical cases remain extant, and such as do might easily be mistaken for French or Low Countries examples. Also in the collection of the Wellcome Historical Medical Museum (from which the fine shagreen case originates) is an Italian silver-mounted tortoiseshell instrument case containing lancets, forceps, a needle, a tongue depressor and a director. This article is dated *circa* 1707, from the contemporary inscription on the base.

In the *Country Life* specimen, there were no fewer than nine instruments—the usual forceps and scissors, directors (guiding devices for bullet probes)—but in addition, a dental scraper for scaling teeth, an ointment spatula, a measuring spoon (for removing ointment from a bottle), and, finally, a tapering tubular 'caustic holder' for holding a stick of silver nitrate at one end, and with a little lidded box for containing red oxide of mercury at the end. There was also a most interesting tongue depressor, which to all but the very initiated, looked like a modern 'all-purpose sardine-tin opener', with an ornamental inverted heart-shaped handle at one end, and a flat vertically pierced blade at the other. The silver mounts on both boxes are very primitively 'scratched' with floral motifs, and the hinges are simple 'book-clasp' types, pinned to the shagreen. Presumably the drawer in the base held the 'edge' tools, to prevent them from loss of sharpness.

2. Boxes with Royal Associations

The detailed inventories of the instrument cases with which the preceding chapter closed have a particular bearing on the first item in this chapter on 'Royal Relics'. It is a most curious phenomenon that many articles which appear gruesome and frightening if belonging to ordinary people, suddenly take on a new and compelling interest if they have belonged at any time in their long history to a Royal personage.

Thus, by the joint courtesies of the Worshipful Company of Barbers and the Worshipful Company of Goldsmiths—in whose custody the article reposes—a most exciting (there can be no other adjective) early 16th century receptacle with elaborate and fascinating Royal associations, appears. This, is, of course, the famous 'Barber-Surgeons' Case' given by King Henry VIII to the Barbers *circa* 1512. Quite apart from the interest of its patron, the article itself is a most superlatively constructed 'box', possessing on the one hand, most elaborate enrichment, and, on the other, a primitiveness which betokens its great age.

The peculiar fascination which surrounds this beautiful instrument case is all the more heightened by the fact, that until the mid-1930's, its very existence was unknown, and, indeed, no mention is made of it in the official History of the Company of Barber-Surgeons. To quote the account relating to the Case issued by the Worshipful Company of Barbers: 'There is every evidence that it was made to the order of Henry VIII, for presentation to the Barbers' Company, who practiced minor surgery as well as the craft of "Barbery", an important body in Henry's day, and of whom he became patron on granting them a charter in 1512. It may have been on the occasion of his Coronation, the tradition being that the City Livery Companies were represented in the Coronation procession and that the official appointed to this duty carried an emblem representative of his trade or guild. Whatever the event or the reason of the gift it was undoubtedly given before 1525 as the Greyhound supporter to the Arms was only used by Henry VIII until that year, when it was replaced by the lion.

The presence on the Case of the enamelled Arms of the Barbers and, below that, separately, the cognizance of the Surgeons' Company, establishes the fact that it was given to these bodies before the granting of the combined Arms in 1540'.

The Account continues: 'this silver Case is in the form of an upright standing box $7\frac{1}{4}$ inches high, is of oblong section $2\frac{1}{4}$ inches by 2 inches at the top and slightly tapering towards the base, from which projects, for a few inches lower, a smaller piece of similar section. The cover is loose but is retained in position by the wood and leather interior which finishes above the lip of the body, thus forming a bezel over which the cover fits. A length of chain fastened at each end to a ring held in the mouth of a lion's mask on both sides of the body passes through rings, attached similarly to the cover, and so further secures the cover in position whilst allowing it to be raised. The corded and moulded borders that outline the case are gilt, leaving the flat surfaces of silver.

On the front of the body of the Box, which has a recess each side, in which are niched and canopied figures of Saint Cosmo and Damien, the Patron Saints of the Barbers' Company, are enamelled the Arms of this Company, viz: Sable a chevron between 3 fleams [a kind of ancient lancet] argent, which were granted to them by Edward IV, in 1462.

On the front of the cover, also enamelled in colour, are the Royal Arms of Henry VIII. Applied in relief are the Greyhound and Dragon Supporters used by Henry VII, and until 1525 by his successor; the whole being surmounted by the Royal Crown. Below the Arms of the Company on the body of the box, and also in relief, is a "spatula surmounted by a rose crowned", a cognizance (device in heraldry borne for distinction by all the retainers of a noble house, whether they bore 'Arms' or not) granted to the Surgeons' Guild by Henry VII in 1492. Being a cognizance, not a Coat-of-Arms, the device is shown thus, instead of in a shield. Under Henry VIII, the Company of Surgeons was incorporated with the Barbers Company and the Arms of the two united. The Companies were again dissolved by an Act of George II, but the Arms of the Barbers Company still retain the charges which properly belong to the Company of Surgeons.

The back of the body is engraved (in a panel) with a subject representative of the Martyrdom of Thomas a Becket, (the choice of subject being strange, for the memory of the Saint was unpopular with the autocratic monarch. Becket had maintained the primacy of spiritual power against the temporal power of the monarchy, whereas Henry had maintained opposite principles when he proclaimed himself supreme head of the English church; it has to be remembered, of course, that this gift was given long before the King's involvement with the

Henry VIII Instrument Case: known as the 'Barber Surgeons' Case'. Parcel-gilt, that is, partially gilt. All sides, the top and base, front and back of the case are illustrated, and the article is fully described in the text.
Unmarked *circa* 1512.
Size: $7\frac{1}{4}$ inches. Top section $2\frac{1}{4}$ inches by 2 inches.
Courtesy of the Worshipful Company of Barbers.

Pope over his Divorce with Queen Catherine of Aragon). On the cover portion is an engraved panel depicting St. George slaying the Dragon.

On the right side it is enriched by engraving in foliate scrolls, and a mask and a figure of Cupid. Below this, in its niche, rests a beautifully modelled figure of St. Catherine, the Saint of Healing. Turning to the left side, a similar style of engraving will be seen, introducing grotesque masks, while below, opposite to St. Catherine, and similarly placed, is a figure of St. John. On the cover section on the same side, around the gilt lion's mask through which the chain passes, are mermen and dolphins.

In red enamel, silver and gilt on the top of the cover, is the Tudor Rose, supported again, as in the case of the Arms, by the Greyhound and Dragon, the whole being surmounted by the Royal Crown. On removing the cover, is revealed a wood and leather fitment with divisions for surgical instruments, which latter unfortunately have not survived'.

It will now be apparent why so much emphasis was placed earlier on the surgical instruments in the shagreen cases; medicine, especially surgical instruments, did not alter very much between the 16th and 17th centuries, and while the instruments contained in the magnificent Barber-Surgeons' Case would probably have been enriched with glowing enamels and inlaid with damscened precious metals, their form and functions would probably have differed little from the silver instruments made almost a century and a half later.

In his wonderful appraisal of *English and Scottish Silver Spoons*, written in collaboration with Mrs. Jane Penrice How, the late Commander G. E. P. How, RN, in dealing with the identities of the Apostles appearing on the 'Barber Surgeons' Case' said the following: 'This quite lovely Mediaeval object is fully described in the *Catalogue of Silver-Work Bronzes Etc.—Lee Collection*, by W. W. Watts, as follows:

"On the front are figures of SS. Cosmo and Damian, patron saints of doctors, whilst between the figures is an enamelled shield of the Arms of the Company granted by Edward IV in 1462. Below the Company's arms is a Spatula surmounted by a crown and Tudor rose—a cognisance granted by Henry VII to the Surgeons' Guild in 1492. On the front also appear the enamelled arms of Henry VII; the royal supporters, a greyhound and dragon, being those in use before 1525 when they were replaced by the lion and unicorn".

Although unmarked, this case can thus be dated with certainty to between the years 1492 (when Henry VII granted the crown and Tudor rose to the Guild) and 1509, the end of the reign of Henry VII.

We are only concerned with the figures on this case, which, as can be seen from the illustration, could easily be adapted as spoon finials, even to the pediments on which they stand. Those here illustrated on the front are the brothers, SS. Damian and Cosmo, Patron Saints of medicine. Both these figures are represented as young unshaven men, one, to dexter, carrying the water bottle in his left hand, and an object not clear, possibly a book, in his right; the other, to sinister, carries the Pot of Ointment in his left hand, his right hand being held across the body, but apparently with intent to hold the draperies rather than in blessing (see St. John on side of the case). No spoons topped with the figures of these Saints are known to exist, or to be mentioned in records, but they may well have been made to special order for members of the Barber Surgeons' fraternity. On the dexter side of the instrument case is the figure of the clean shaven St. John, the Cup held in his left hand, the right hand held across the body. Here, as with SS. Damian and Cosmo on the front of the case, the figure could easily be adapted as a spoon finial, and in all probability the model is one used for the purpose in the late 15th-early 16th century . . . On the sinister side of the case is the figure of St. Catherine, known from wills and inventories to have been employed as a finial on spoons though no genuine English examples so topped are at present recorded.

Here the beautifully modelled Saint carries her emblem of the Sword, apparently sheathed, in her right hand; one of the quillons (the arms forming the cross-guard of the sword) would seem to have been broken off. At her feet is the Wheel, the emblem of her martyrdom, and in her left hand she carries a book. This model may well have been one of those used as spoon finials in the early 16th century'.

This excellent analysis of the figures on the Case could hardly have been bettered; coming as it did from the greatest authority on Apostle Terminals, it must be considered the final word on the identity of the Saints and their Emblems.

Something ought to be said about the Barber-Surgeons themselves: until quite

Note
Commander How's assertion that the Case can be dated 'with certainty' to between 1492 and 1509 (which would make it of Henry VII provenance) and the official text issued by the Worshipful Company of Barbers ascribing it to *circa* 1512 (which would date it as of Henry VIII origin) are not, in reality, greatly contradictory: the former is based on the Commander's great scholarship in relation to the types of terminals on spoons, the latter on the type of 'cognizance' applied on the front of the case. Either way, there is a divergence of three years, which period does not materially alter the approximate dating.

recently, it was widely believed that the Barbers were merely itinerant mendicants, practising 'quack' medicine, while at the same time pursuing their normal trade; modern research has established that many of these 'Barber-Surgeons' were, in fact, educated men of medicine, who studied and spoke Latin, and, within the limits of their day, knew as much about primitive surgery as many accredited surgeons. Their vocation has always attracted much attention and thus a 'tradition' has sprung up around them of haphazard 'surgery'. It has to be remembered that some of the accepted methods in use in the late 16th century

were of equal barbarism but people who had little to lose underwent 'operations' from which, surprisingly, quite a few survived.

On the 30th January 1649 (1648 according to the contemporary reckoning) King Charles the First suffered the supreme penalty. With his death, this sad and often macabre tale begins.

The embalmed remains were privately interred, after much delay: the

The King's Hair

Puritans, fearing that were the exact site of the tomb known, it might become a martyr's shrine, insisted on a secret interment, unattended by burial rites or other ceremonies. The King's courtiers were eventually granted grudging permission to bury him in St. George's Chapel, Windsor, in a vault already occupied by King Henry VIII and his third wife, Queen Jane Seymour.

When, after the Restoration, Charles II would have liked to re-inter his Royal Father in a place more befitting the martyred King, it was found, inexplicably, that the exact site of the tomb had been forgotten: whether as a result of the mutilations which the Puritans had made to the Chapel, or because

in their haste the courtiers had overlooked to mark the spot, is not known. There the matter languished for another one hundred and sixty years.

It was not an altogether unhappy accident, therefore, that during reconstruction work in St. George's Chapel in the year 1813, the workmen engaged in the task of building a mausoleum in the Tomb-house, accidentally breached one of the walls of a vault. They found therein not only the coffins of King Henry VIII and his Queen, but also a third, covered in a black velvet pall, and bearing a leaden plate inscribed 'King Charles 1648'.

Top row:
Left
George III lancet case: covered in shagreen with silver mounts. Containing two lancets.
Maker: John Reily, London 1797.
Size: 3 inches by 1½ inches.

Centre
Victorian lancet case: silver-gilt and engine-turned with 'basketweave' motifs and with cast foliate borders. Containing one lancet.
Makers: Taylor and Perry, Birmingham 1845.
Size: 3 inches by 1¼ inches.

Right
Victorian lancet case: of shallow type, engraved with 'abstract' motif and with reeded rim. Containing two lancets.
No maker's mark, Birmingham 1843.
Size: 3 inches by 1½ inches.

Centre row:
Left
Victorian lancet case: of rectangular 'sliding lid' variety, engraved with foliate motifs on engine-turned 'fox's head' ground. Containing two lancets.
Maker: Thomas Dones, Birmingham 1853.
Size: 3 inches by 1¼ inches.
Thomas Dones entered his mark at Birmingham in 1850.

Right
Victorian lancet case: silver-gilt and enriched overall with scrolling foliate motifs and with cast foliate borders. Containing six lancets.
Maker: Joseph Willmore, Birmingham 1841.
Size: 3 inches by 2¼ inches.

Bottom row:
Left
William IV lancet case: engraved with foliate motifs. Containing two lancets.
Makers: Taylor and Perry, Birmingham 1836.
Size: 3 inches by 1½ inches.

Centre
Victorian lancet case: the sides bright-cut with foliate motifs on a 'double-dot' scored ground. Containing six lancets.
Makers: Taylor and Perry, Birmingham 1845.
Size: 3 inches by 2¼ inches.

Right
William IV lancet case: silver-gilt and engine-turned with 'basketweave' motifs and cast foliate borders, and with 'stand-away' hinge'. Containing two lancets.
Makers: Ledsam, Vale and Wheeler, Birmingham 1830.
Size: 3 inches by 1½ inches.
Courtesy of the Wellcome Medical Historical Museum.

Sir Henry Halford

It is at this juncture, that the name of Sir Henry Halford makes its appearance: as it is one which will recur constantly in this account, it is necessary to cite something of its pedigree and associations with the Martyr King.

Of Royal Descent and Royalist Ancestry

In addition to being the Physician to King George III, and President of the Royal College of Physicians (and thus eminently suited to preside at a Royal exhumation) Halford (1766–1844) was also a scion of a noble Royalist family, which, furthermore, bore a direct lineal descent from King Henry III (1216–72), his own position being 18th in succession. His ancestor, Sir Richard Halford, was a loyal supporter of King Charles, who knighted him in 1641. During his campaign at Naseby, Charles slept at Wistow, Halford's Leicestershire estate for a few days before the Battle, and would have returned there after his defeat had he not been 'so closely pursued that he did not dare to stay to have his saddle changed'. The King's saddle and that of Prince Rupert, who accompanied him, was left at Wistow.

It will accordingly be apparent that Henry Halford was considered no mere medical practitioner, but a staunch Royalist in his own right. The invitation to attend that historic exhumation on the first Thursday of April, 1813 was spontaneously extended, but might have been less enthusiastic had there been a premonition that Halford would take advantage of an unhappy and distressing accident to despoil the sacred remains of his liege.

The Exhumation

Halford himself published an innocuous account of the opening of the King's casket, which described in detail the similarity of the features with those in Van Dyck's famous portrait of Charles I—thus proving beyond all possible doubt that at long last his remains had been discovered—a description of the burial-vault, and a list of those present at the opening: The Prince Regent, The Duke of Cumberland, the Dean of Windsor (in whose care the remains reposed), Count Munster, Benjamin Charles Stevenson, Esq., and Halford himself. Stevenson was also a descendant of a loyal Royalist family.

Fortunately for the sake of historical accuracy, an anonymous contemporary account described what actually took place. The exhumation, contrary to popular belief, was not the result of a carefully planned arrangement, but one made on the spur of the moment; when the Prince Regent was informed that a casket bearing King Charles's name had been discovered in St. George's

William IV oval elliptical snuffbox: with delicate foliate rim and reeded sides, and gold rim to the original bevelled glass lid. Under the glass is a lock of King Charles I's hair (fully described in *The King's Hair* in this chapter) on a faded blue velvet pad. With 'stand-away' hinged lid.
Maker: James Scott, Dublin 1831.
Size: 3¾ inches by 2¼ inches by 1⅛ inches deep.

Chapel, he immediately adjourned to the vault together with such gentlemen as were in his company (pausing only to summon Halford and the Dean). The only persons available to open the casket were a plumber and his lad, who happened to be working in the precincts at the time, and to these unskilled artisans fell the task of removing the King's cere-cloth, and exposing the Royal visage. This delicate operation was accomplished with a chisel! The plumber, who, poor man, was undoubtedly extremely nervous, obeying the Prince's instructions to lift out the head, did so, and promptly dropped it onto the floor, whereupon the Prince swore at him and left the chamber in disgust. Halford's subsequent claim that a piece of bone had remained unnoticed when the casket was closed up again, and that the Prince Regent, rather than disturb the remains, presented him with the relic, is thus manifestly shown to be untrue.

Halford's Relic-Snatching

Now, Henry Halford, who was disliked by many for his hauteur to inferiors and subservience to superiors, and known accordingly as the 'Eel-backed Baronet', had one failing above all others: he was an inveterate gossip and loved to indulge in anecdote. The opportunity thus offered to him by the absence of the Prince was too tempting, and he led a general 'relic-snatching'. He removed

William III oval elliptical snuffbox: with 'stand-away' hinge, the domed lid exceptionally engraved with symbolic Royalist subjects. With disguised 'inner lid' depicting 'Dogs gnawing bones' motif in partially cast high relief.
Maker: Lawrence Coles, London 1697.
Size: 3 inches by 2 inches by ⅛ inch deep.
This box is fully analysed and discussed under the title 'A Jacobite Relic'.

the King's fourth cervical vertebra, and portions of the hair of the beard and head. Stevenson went even further and desecrated Henry VIII's casket (which was much decayed) removing a tooth of the Mighty Tudor.

Oddly enough, the Prince Regent, who must have known that something unethical had occurred after he left the vault, as he himself had obtained a lock of King Charles's hair to give to his daughter Princess Charlotte, said nothing to Halford; in fact, he gave him his 'Certificate of Authenticity' when the account was published. Apparently Halford was not despised by his contemporaries for removing portions of the Royal hair, as this practice was quite widespread during the preceding centuries—in 1784, for instance, the body of Mary Tudor was disturbed, and lengths of her hair two feet in length were annexed. These were subsequently sold at the Duke of Buckingham's sale at Stowe in 1848. Similarly, in 1786, the remains of Queen Katherine Parr were disturbed and various relics removed.

What really enraged the Royal Family and indeed all decent citizens, was Halford's deplorable practice of wearing the King's vertebra on a fob-chain and displaying it to all and sundry. He was particularly fond of shocking his guests at dinner by showing them the relic and saying 'Here is a piece of Charles the First'.

The Return of the Relic

To the consternation of his friends, Halford made no attempt to deny the allegations that he had behaved unethically. In fact, he continued to flaunt the relic, and even had a gold-lined box made for it, with a suitable Latin inscription. It was only many years after his death that his grandson, Sir Henry St. John Halford, deciding that it was time for the relic to be returned to its original source, offered it back to the Queen. Sir Henry was summoned to Marlborough House, where the Prince of Wales received it from him on behalf of the Queen, and, 'by saying no word of thanks and turning his back, made it plain, to the

great distress of the dear old man, that he supposed the relic to have been improperly come by'.

The final chapter of this sorry tale was written in a brief statement in *The Times*, 17th December, 1888: 'The Prince of Wales on Thursday visited St. George's Chapel, Windsor, and replaced in the vault containing the coffin of Charles I certain relics of that monarch which had been removed during some investigations more than seventy years ago. These relics having ultimately come into the possession of the Prince of Wales, he decided, with the sanction of the Queen, to replace them in the vault from which they had been taken, but not to disturb the coffin of the King. The Dean of Windsor was present'.

In 1964, an Irish snuffbox made in Dublin in 1831 was noted. The lid was formed as a glassed-in compartment containing a lock of greying-auburn hair resting on a blue velvet pad. Inside the box, written on a small piece of card, and stuck into the bottom with mucilage, was the following inscription: 'The hair beneath the glass lid of this box is that of King Charles the First. It was obtained when the coffin of that King was opened in 1813: after a search had been made for it in St. George's Chapel, Windsor, and was given to my father J. H. Cochrane by a relative of one who was present at the time. HLC'. (It is obvious that the aforesaid gentleman had the Snuffbox specially made to accommodate the Relic).

The ascription was extremely interesting, but was it conclusive? After all, the Victorians were notorious for their fondness of ascribing relics to various mythical celebrities, and this specimen could have been purely apocryphal. It was therefore decided to submit a minute sample to modern chemical analysis. After much difficulty (no-one felt sufficiently competent to undertake such a delicate task) the services of an exceptionally distinguished Dermatologist (who had made a study of this very subject, namely, the analysis of ancient, even pre-historic human hair) were obtained.

Having found him, what properties was he to look for? Well, firstly, the approximate age of the hair, and secondly, the presence on the hair of any embalming fluids. It was known, from contemporary records that the King had been embalmed by the 'Chirurgeon Trapham' in 1649, and that it was possible to discount the possibility that the hair was not that of the King, it being quite unthinkable to disinter an ordinary embalmed body and remove from it any portion of the hair. After massive research in the Reading Room of the British Museum, it was discovered that the contemporary methods of embalming would have involved the use of certain resins and waxes, and upon receiving this information, the analyst was able to proceed. No more than three hairs were removed from the lock, and upon these, the fascinating modern scientific processes were performed.

The Analyst's Report
A Report on a sample of Human Hair said to have come from Charles the First
'The hairs were examined microscopically to determine possible chemical alteration as a result of ageing and the use of embalming preparations. The hairs were also examined to find out whether they were from the scalp or the beard. The possibility that they had been dyed was also investigated.

Appearance by Fluorescence Microscopy
The hairs when examined microscopically under ultra-violet light had a brighter self fluorescence than modern human hair. This bright fluorescence was reduced in hairs soaked overnight in an organic solvent, xylene, to remove embalming substances. Some resins, such as canada balsam, have a similar blue self fluorescence, and this suggests that the hairs were treated with some resinous substance, possibly rosin. I have not, however, examined the fluorescence of rosin.

Air bubbles are found in the centre of old hairs, but none were seen in this sample. Air normally enters through the damaged hair cuticle; this may, however, have been prevented in this instance by substances applied to the hair during embalming.

Fluorescence of Hair stained in 0.1% Acridine Orange
Hairs stained in this fluorescent dye and then examined microscopically under ultra-violet light showed a patchy orange fluorescence. This indicates damage to the chemical structure of the hair mainly confined to the hair cuticle. The effect was very similar to the changes we have found in hair from dynastic Egyptian mummies.

Hair Colour
The hair is lighter brown than the scalp hair shown in portraits of Charles the First in the National Portrait Gallery although the beard is shown as a lighter

reddish brown. Since, however, the present specimen appears to be scalp hair, it must have faded if it came from Charles the First. [*Note: The learned Doctor has obviously overlooked that these old portraits in the Gallery are uncleaned, and that the colour thus shown to be darker than the specimen of hair, was originally much lighter in life.*]

Some fading sometimes occurs in old hair, and we have found that modern dark hair became slightly darker in colour after being buried for eighteen months in soil.

If at any time in its history this sample had been exposed to light, as in a show case, this could cause fading from a darker to a somewhat lighter brown colour.

I soaked some hairs overnight in warm dilute hydrochloric acid which should remove henna. As the colour of the hair was unchanged after this treatment, the hair was probably not dyed.

Conclusion

These findings are consistent with the view that the hair sample is old and that it has in the past been treated with some embalming preparation. It appears to be scalp hair and is not dyed. The only inconsistent feature is its light colour, but this could have resulted from fading. Therefore, I believe that this hair sample could have come from Charles the First'.

Stuart Relics

Not surprisingly, there are few fully authenticated Stuart Relics. The important Stuart Exhibition held in London at the New Gallery in 1889 contained many genuine relics, among them the pitiful possessions given by King Charles to his faithful Groom of the Bedchamber, John Ashburnham, on the day of execution, including the King's watch and shirt. Other relics included the blue silk vest in which the King met his death, and more impersonal relics, such as books, ribbons, medallions and portraits.

Of the pieces of hair known to have been annexed by Halford, four are traceable: Lord Ashburnham and Sir Benjamin Stevenson both had specimens, as had William Barclay Squire, Esq., and Sir Walter Scott, who begged a piece from Halford through the eminent physician Matthew Baillie, and wore it in a gold ring for some years.

A Jacobite Relic

It is entirely natural, perhaps, for every researcher, to dream of the one outstanding item which will make all the back-breaking work worth while. Frequently, after months of deep and massive searching, very little emerges; sometimes, as in this present work, there are 'untapped' subjects galore! While it would be quite impossible for the writer to select any one item as his favourite (they are all of his own selection, although he was greatly assisted by the many owners), his very strong 'Royalist' sympathies (the section on 'The King's Hair', for instance, took nearly six months of devoted labour to 'uncover the dust of centuries') have attracted him to the oval engraved snuffbox which is the subject of this analysis.

This work is made all the more attractive by the fact that the hard work has already been done: an opinion on the superb 'emblemata' on the lid was sought from a leading Cambridge scholar, who is *the* authority on the Stuart Period.

A tentative Opinion from Prof. J. H. Plumb, Litt.D., F.S.A.,
Vice Master of Christ's College, Cambridge, who writes:

'I have spent a fascinating weekend on the box. It is obviously engraved with emblems which relate directly to the Stuarts. Presumably, the intention, if the box can be dated on stylistic grounds to about 1700, is to imply that what happened to Charles II would probably apply to James II. So, probably, the box belonged to an ardent Jacobite. I read the emblems in the following way:

The son (pun on the 'sun') of Charles I (who is clearly the central figure at the top of the box. The fact that he is unclothed shows that he is in heaven (and, of course, a martyr) will return or emerge (as the moon is doing from the eclipse) from the Boscobel Oak (the oak tree with the Welsh mountains behind, which was commonly used as a symbol for Charles II at the time of the Commonwealth) to his kingdom (indicated by the engraved city on the right) or this might read from Breda (I have not seen an engraving of this city, but it might be related to a city with twin spires) and restore the succession (the crown), royal authority (orb), the church (mitre), bring peace (the sceptre laid across the sword) restore the coinage (the bits of gold on the table), and hang (the halter) his enemies.

And the rest of the story is told on the chased (inner) lid. There is the picture of a peaceful and plentiful countryside and obviously the dogs are gnawing the bones of the king's enemies. The fact of the guineas on the table, suggests, I

think, that the box can be dated just after 1696 when the re-coinage by the government of William III created great difficulty for most people and brought about a chronic shortage of cash. Also I think that this emblematic description of restoration of the Stuarts is cast in an historic form so that it could not be regarded as treasonable. It could be argued that it only depicted what had happened in 1660, although the implication, of course, is clear enough: what happened once might happen again'.

It will be recalled that in chapter one, in the section dealing with hinges the type of Dutch 'wide flange' hinge is discussed. This present oval box with the 'Jacobite Emblems' is of a very similar type, and this fact, in addition to Dr. Plumb's reference to 'Breda' as a 'city with twin spires', (Breda was a fortified town in Holland from which, in 1660, Charles II stated his conditions for his return to the English Monarchy) a careful comparison with Plate liii, No. 3 in the *Medallic Illustrations* which shows a beautifully struck silver medal commemorating the Peace of Breda, 1667, depicts this city almost exactly as it appears on the lid of the box, with the exception, of course, of the primitiveness of the latter and the elaborate conception of the former.

This apparent Dutch provenance could relieve several puzzling factors: one, the type of engraving: who was there in England at the turn of the 17th century who could have undertaken such clear 'emblemata' with impunity but an artist of the Dutch School? Further, in view of Dr. Plumb's carefully implied suggestion of 'the treasonable implications' of producing such a box in England, perhaps the article was made in Holland to an English commission? Secondly, the un-English type of hinge, and thirdly, and perhaps most important of all, the vagueness of the London hall-marks struck inside the base of the container. The maker's mark is barely discernible, but the date-letter, while it is unquestionably there, can hardly be seen at all. It is as if a sympathetic Assay-master struck, or ordered to

be struck, a date-letter for posterity's sake alone; the mark could hardly have become so rubbed in an otherwise impeccably preserved silver-gilt interior.

Yet another enigma lies within the clandestine or 'hidden' inner lid of the box which has a high domed outer lid to accommodate this. The work, although resembling 'casting' is not completely solid, but is wrought as a partially-cast plaque in high relief, somewhat reminiscent of Benjamin Pyne's 'religious subjects'; this plaque is unmarked, but one thing is quite apparent: whoever made this outstanding receptacle was a Master Boxmaker, and to any lover of the House of Stuart, it is a wonderful relic indeed.

Counter boxes have received careful attention above, and Simon van de Passe's method of 'die-stamping' was also included in the survey. The pierced-top counter box illustrated is but one of the many such 'British Worthies' series, but differs in one important respect: it has, as *its* subject a hitherto untraced portrait of the youthful Charles II. The disc which enriches the circularly pierced box depicts a young man with a large nose and flowing locks (in profile it is not unlike Samuel Cooper's famous miniature of 'Charles II when young' which is figure 23 in the *Illustrated Handlist of Miniature Portraits and Silhouettes* of the

Charles II pierced circular counterbox: the lid repoussé with bust of the King, the sides pierced with foliate motifs, engraved on base with 'tulip' motif and contemporary initials. Containing contemporary game-counters by Simon van de Passe. Unmarked, *circa* 1660. Size: 1 inch in diameter by 1½ inches deep.

A Counter Box Showing Charles II

William III 'Boscobel Oak' snuffbox: of oval shape, with reeded rim and 'stand-away' hinge. The lid inset with oaken panel upon which is pinned a 'cut-out' depicting the scene in Boscobel Wood, with Charles II sitting in the oak tree, while armed riders prowl below. A cherub offers the King three crowns, symbolic of the Three Kingdoms. The 'motto ribbon' is empty.
Unmarked, *circa* 1700, probably engraved by Netherlands artist.
(This article is mentioned in the text).
Size: 3¾ inches by 2½ inches.

The Boscobel Oak Boxes

Victoria and Albert Museum). Deeply penetrating research has revealed no other source for this portrait: certainly, it does not appear in *Medallic Illustrations*, and other similar publications.

The term 'unique' is a very dangerous expression, and it may well be, in spite of the many learned opinions which were sought and obtained, all of negative form, that there may be hundreds of these 'unknown portraits'. Suffice it to say that of the many leading authorities who were consulted, only one very senior member of a famous numismatical house was able, at the very first glance, to exclaim 'Without a doubt, this is the young Charles II'. Perhaps there will be dissenters, but such is the price of knowledge; without contradiction, there can be no learning!

The 'die-struck' counters contained in the box are of the common variety, and of the five specimens shown, four are clearly identifiable: reading from left to right: Queen Elizabeth of Bohemia, the daughter of King James I of England, King John (the reversed counter is that of King Edward III), King Edward IV, and King Henry II.

A great deal has already been written about these finely engraved, somewhat mournful relics of the tribulations of the young King Charles II following the martyrdom of his Royal father. The present specimen was selected for the beautiful clarity of the engraving (which follows the traditional iconography) and, once again, in pursuance of the theory that 'stand-away' hinges betoken Dutch or Low Countries influence. Moreover, the 'motto-ribbon' at the base of the lid is empty, and this could suggest that the engraver was ignorant of the subject-matter and was merely copying the portrait from another version. An interesting example of this 'ignorance' occurs on one of the oval 'spiceboxes' illustrated elsewhere, where the obviously English engraver, copying a French mottor "Vn Sevl Me Blesse"—'One alone injures me' has heavily incised the 'l' in

'Blesse' to make the word read 'Beesse', which makes no sense at all . . .

The story of the Boscobel Oak has been retailed often enough, but not, perhaps in the words of the original biography by Thomas Blount (1618–1679), published 1660.

'About three of the clock on Saturday morning [September 6th 1651], being come near the house [Boscobel], Richard [Penderel] left his Majesty in the wood, whilst he went in to see if no souldiers were there or other danger; where he found Col. William Carliss (who had seen, not the last man born, but the last man kild, at Worcester, and) who, having with much difficulty, made his escape from thence; was got into his own neighbor-hood, and for some time concealing himself in Boscobel Wood, was come that morning to the house to get some relief of William Penderel, his old acquaintance.

Richard having acquainted the Col. that the king was in the wood, the Col. with Willaim and Richard goe presently thither to give their attendance, where they found his Majesty sitting on the root of a tree, who was glad to see the Col. and came with them into the house, and did there eat bread and cheese heartily, and (as an extraordinary) William Penderels wife made his Majesty a posset, of thin milk and small beer, and got ready some warm water to wash his feet, not onely extreme dirty, but much galled with travail.

The Col. pull'd off his Majesties shoos, which were full of gravel, and stockens which were very wet, and there being no other shoos in the house, that would fit his Majesty, the good wife put some hot embers in those to dry them, whilst his Majesties feet were washing and his stockens shifted.

Being thus a little refreshed, the Col. perswaded his Majesty to go back into the wood (supposing it safer than the house) where the Colonel made choice of a thick leafed oak, into which both William and Richard hel'd both the King and the Col. and brought them such provision as they could get, with a cushion for his Majesty to sit on; in this oak they continued most part of that day, and the Col. humbly desired his Majesty (who had taken little or no rest the two preceding nights) to seat himself as easily as he could in the tree, and rest his head on the Colonels lap, who was watchfull that his Majesty might not fall; and in this posture his Majesty slumber'd away some part of the day, and bore all these hardships and afflictions with incomparable patience'.

Blount epitomised Colonel Carliss (sometimes called 'Careless' by later biographers) thus: 'This Col. William Carlis was born at Bromhall in Stafford-shire, within two miles of Boscobel, of good parentage, is a person of approved valor, and was engag'd all along in the first war for his late Majesty of happy memory, and since his death has been no less active for his Majesty that now is; for which and his particular service and fidelity before mentioned, his Majesty has been pleased by letters patent under the great seal of England to give him, by the name of *William Carlos* (which in Spanish signifies *Charls*), this very honorable coat of armes (illustrated, and analysed thus: 'He bears vpon an Oake proper, in a Feild Or, a Fesse Gules, charged with 3 Regal Crowns of ye second: by the name of Carlos. And for his Creast a Civic Crown, or Oaken Garland, with a Sword and Scepter crossed through it Saltierwise') *in perpetuam rei memoriam*, as 'tis expressed in the letters patent'.

In conclusion, there is a very touching little verse engraved on a copper-gilt oval pendant in the Victoria and Albert Museum, one side of which bears the Arms described above, the other a finely engraved portrait showing both the King and Carlos in the Oak, and engraved inside the following:

> 'Renowned Carlos! thou hast won the day
> (loyalty lost) by helping Charles away
> From Kings' blood-thirsty rebels jn a night
> Made black with rage of thieves & hell's dispight,
> Live! King-loved Sowle thy fame by euer spoke,
> By all whilst England beares a Royall Oake'.

Royal Portrait Pomanders

There is no attempt, here, to accord any direct Royal provenance with the rare 'globular pomanders' which bear finely engraved portraits of English Kings and Queens on the 'loculi' or segments. The present specimen is of the 'six-segment' variety, and shows six English monarchs: one each from the Houses of Lancaster and York, and four from the House of the Tudors. These are, in chronological order:

Henry IV—1367–1413
Edward IV—1442–1483
Henry VII—1457–1509
Henry VIII—1491–1547
Edward VI—1537–1553
Elizabeth I—1533–1603

It is not thought that there was anything particularly special about these 'Royal Portrait' pomanders—they were probably wrought as 'Patriotic Mementoes', in much the same manner as portraits of The Evangelists appeared on German specimens, but what is of interest is that of the six monarchs depicted on the English example, three, at least, are known to have been particularly interested in perfumes, namely, Henry VIII (whose recipe for a pomander containing ambergris is among the Ashmolean MSS), Edward VI, who liked rose perfume, and Queen Elizabeth, who likewise had a special fondness for the rose, which would seem to have been the favourite perfume of the Tudors.

While there were, of course, many bejewelled and finely engraved plain pomanders'—they were engraved by hand—and it is probable that their question, in this instance, of the method used in engraving these 'portrait pomanders'—they were engraved by hand—and it is probably that their embellishers copied the work of such master-engravers as Renold Elstrack (working 1598–1623), who engraved most of the plates for the famous *Bazili-ωogia . . . the true and lively Effigies of all our English Kings . . . printed for H. Holland and sold by Compton Holland,* 1618. The 'Effigies' were most beautifully engraved, and Miss Helen Farquhar (*vide supra*) thought that some, at least, of the Passe counters, were based on them. It would be too much to seek to ascribe the ornament on these 'Portrait Pomanders' to the hand of Simon van de Passe, although he could have engraved some to important commissions.

Some 'Portrait Pomanders' are very finely engraved, others quite coarsely, and it is highly probably that emigré Dutch engravers were busily turning out these new 'novelties': as one contemporary 20th century expert has remarked : 'Dutch engravers were ten a penny in the late 16th–early 17th centuries!'

The subject of Pomanders having been treated extensively (vide *Investing in Silver* pp.105-107) it is not proposed to repeat published material, but there are some aspects which have come to notice, and are therefore included here. The late Director of the Wellcome Medical Museum, Dr. E. Ashworth Underwood stated that 'a pomander with six sections enabled six substances to be inhaled simultaneously'. This would certainly explain the absence of 'slides' on the present example, and why many pomanders noted appear never to have had these 'slides' or covers, or any provision for these, to enclose the segments.

The very early prototype of the pomander would seem to be the German *Bisamapfel*, or 'musk-ball' which Hugh Tait mentions in another learned article in the November 1963 issue of *The Connoisseur*, dealing with 'an anonymous loan to the British Museum of Renaissance Jewellery'. Mr. Tait specifies that 'one of the earliest mediaeval pomanders of this segmental type is preserved in the Bayerisches Nationalmuseum in Munich . . . made in the Rhineland 1470', but John Timbs's *Nooks and Corners of English Life*, published in 1867 refers to an inventory of Henry V, date A.D. 1423 which enumerated a 'musk-ball of gold, weighing *eleven pounds*, and another of silver-gilt. Finally, Giles Merton, writing in *Argentor* 1948, stated his opinion that 'pomanders were not always used for the purpose of holding perfume. Many of the Renaissance pomanders were pear-shaped and *held cosmetics* in their divisions'.

Perhaps the most essential requisite which the researcher into the historic past should possess is that combination of healthy curiosity and passion to 'dot all the 'i's, and cross all the 't's—which can become both the bane and salvation of his work—and the intelligent use of which can lead him into all sorts of fascinating adventures.

The present writer's great obsession is the identification, as far as is humanly possible, of the many themes appearing within these pages, and thus he found himself intrigued by the historical background to the cast oval plaque set within the lid of the silver-gilt casket bearing Queen Charlotte's Royal Cypher. Expert opinion was sought, but the scene remained obstinately obscure; famous battles of the period were scrutinised (the subject appears to contain warriors as well as the three central mounted figures), prints and drawings involving famous historical *causes célèbres* cast no light on the enigma. It seemed that Thomas Heming, the maker of the casket had invented an ornamental theme without any factual basis.

Having exhausted the normal sources of enquiry, it became necessary to delve deeper into the matter: the first and most pressing problem was how a Royal relic had left its original surroundings and had passed into lay possession.

It became expedient to search Exhibition Catalogues and learned articles, and one fact of passing interest did emerge: the casket had been shown in May 1939 at an Exhibition entitled 'The Age of Queen Charlotte', held at the Luton Museum. Various works of art, including ceramics, furniture and silver were exhibited by several world-famous firms, and beyond the customary description and a brief note on the rococo style in which the article was wrought, nothing more was added.

The enigma was finally solved through an article by the scholarly expert on antique porcelain, Dr. Bellamy Gardner who, in the July 1939 issue of *The Connoisseur* wrote of 'Rare Souvenirs of King George III and Queen Charlotte', and cited several rare items of Chelsea Porcelain which had been '*sold among Her Majesty's effects by Messrs Christie in the year 1819*'. Armed with this information it was possible to trace the rare early catalogue (a slim volume, labelled simply 'Queen Charlotte's Catalogue, 1819') and to track down the 'Superb Service of silver-gilt Plate', (sic) which comprised thirty articles of a Toilet Service in a red leather case, lined with green velvet.

Among the more important pieces were a mirror, a ewer and basin, several circular boxes and salvers on 'small feet', and a '*pair of large scalloped Toilet Boxes and Covers with roses and flowers in high relief, on four feet*'. In accordance with contemporary practice, neither the name of the maker nor the date of manufacture was given. Now, the backbone of research is comparative correlation with other published works, and in an article in the July 1965 issue of *Apollo Magazine*, A. V. B. Norman, writing of 'An Augsburg Travelling Service', stated (*inter alia*) that the 'Zoffany Portrait of Queen Charlotte at her dressing-table', in the Royal Collections at Windsor '*shows five boxes in use*'. Again, it was

Above
Charles I pomander: of sexagonal 'apple' variety, parcel-gilt on central column and with screw-down lid. Scratched all over with 'debased laurel' motifs. On cast collet foot and with suspensory loop on the closing screw. Unmarked, *circa* 1630.
Size: 2½ inches by 18 inches.
Courtesy of the Wellcome Medical Historical Museum.

Queen Charlotte's Casket

Above and on next page
George III silver-gilt rectangular toilet casket: this Royal Relic belonged to Queen Charlotte, consort of King George III and is engraved with her personal cypher inside the lid. The rococo body is enriched with repoussé floral sprays and 'scroll and beaded foliate' motifs on the four scroll-terminal feet. The lid is embellished with shell, foliate and gadroon motifs, and set in centre with cast pictorial plaque within an oval laurel wreath cartouche. The lid is of the 'rising domical' variety, and has a concealed 'integral hinge'. The subject of the plaque is fully discussed under the heading of 'Queen Charlotte's Casket'.
Maker: Thomas Heming, the Royal Goldsmith, London, 1771.
Size: 8 inches by 5 inches by 4 inches deep.

Left
Victorian silver-gilt sexagonal pomander: finely cast and chased with foliate motifs, the hinges of the 'three-lugged' variety. The spherical cap and screw surmounted by a suspensory loop. The six *loculi* or segments set with turquoises.
Maker: Robert Thornton, London, 1867.
Size: 3 inches by 1⅜ inches in diameter.
All portions marked with lion passant.

a simple matter to trace Zoffany's portrait (and hope, incidentally, alas, in vain, that the cataloguer might say something about the plaques), but from a close examination of the portrait which showed the Queen at a draped dressing-table, in company of the Prince of Wales and the Duke of York, painted at Old Buckingham House, *circa* 1766, it became obvious that the toilet articles which she was using were not of the same rococo style as the present casket, but from another service, also mentioned in the Christie Catalogue of 1819, which was more in keeping with a German oval style.

As is well-known, the Court Goldsmith to George III in the third quarter of the 18th century was Thomas Heming, and A. G. Grimwade, FSA, writing on 'Royal Toilet Services in Scandinavia', published in the April 1956 issue of *The Connoisseur*, described and illustrated an almost identical casket which was part of a toilet service made by Heming for the Queen of Denmark, Caroline Matilda, posthumous daughter of Frederick, Prince of Wales and sister of George III, in 1766. On close examination, the caskets greatly resemble the present specimen, with the exception, perhaps, that the former are somewhat longer and shallower, and that instead of the cast plaque inset on the lid, have cast floral motifs.

In writing of yet another Heming service made for a nobleman in 1768, Mr. Grimwade made the point that 'Heming obviously used the mouldings of the Royal Service (belonging to Queen Caroline Matilda) when the Williams-Wynne service was ordered two years later . . . since he must have been aware that the earlier service was across the seas, he would have felt safe from incurring any suggestion that he had tarnished the lustre of the Royal prototype by producing what is virtually a copy. The use of the existing mouldings must, of course, have made the production of the second service both speedier and cheaper. Heming's profit on this may well have been larger in consequence'. Judging by the almost exact duplication which appears on Queen Charlotte's casket, dated 1771, it would be safe to assert that Heming used the same mouldings yet again, and, what is more, having already used them in the production, only three years earlier, of a service for a noble *English* family (not one beyond the seas), did not hesitate to reproduce them once more, but this time for his chief Patroness, the Queen of England herself!

Within this apparent duplicity may lie the answer to the original question: 'what is the subject of the cast plaque on the lid of the casket?' For a clearer explanation, it becomes necessary to know something of the background of Queen Charlotte herself. Writing in 1899, Percy Fitzgerald, in a wholly masterful and interesting account of the life of 'The Good Queen Charlotte', cited a very important incident in the future Queen of England's early life, and one which must have made a great impression on her, as indeed, it made an impression on the English court, and probably eventually led to her marriage with King George III.

Sophia Charlotte had been born in May, 1744 in the North German Duchy of Mecklenburg-Strelitz. She was the niece of the fourth Duke, Adolphus Frederick, and, says Fitzgerald 'was carefully educated, was fond of botany and natural history, devoted to music: she was a good housewife, and skilful and laborious at her needle. Above all, she was reared in principles of the strictest piety and morality'.

Fitzgerald continues: 'The almost pastoral happiness of the little court at Strelitz had been rudely disturbed by the wars between the Great Frederick (Frederick the Great) and the Empress Maria Theresa, which was to prove disastrous for the small German territories, which he overran with his armies and pillaged and laid waste. His excuse was that they would not join him in the contest. The little Duchy of Mecklenburg-Strelitz suffered cruelly: contributions were levied, the young men were forced into the king's army, furniture and property plundered; even the churches were despoiled. After the great defeat of Daun (Field-marshal—1705–66) at Torgau in 1760 the whole of Germany seemed to be at the conqueror's mercy: so desperate was the outlook, that an extraordinary step was taken by the second of the young princesses then at Strelitz, and which was to determine her future destiny. As the victory seemed to portend a new series of horrors and despoilings, *she addressed an earnest letter to Frederick, describing the sufferings of her country and appealing to his mercy and forbearance.* This was, continues Fitzgerald, 'an exceptional step in one so young, she was then only sixteen—and was as timely as it was efficacious'.

The letter is too long to quote in full, but contains such imploring visions as: 'It was but a few years ago that this territory wore the most pleasing appearance. The country was cultivated, the peasant looked cheerful, and the towns abounded with riches and festivity. What an alteration at present from such a charming scene. I am not expert at description, nor can my fancy add any horrors to the picture; but surely even conquerors themselves would weep at the hideous prospects now before me'. The viciousness of the soldiery and the confusion and the horrors are emphasised. 'It was noted' says Fitzgerald, 'that almost immediately after this letter was despatched, a complete change took place in the Prussian king's system. A missive to General de Ziethen (1699–1786) enjoined order and regularity in the conduct of the army. The king, indeed, was so pleased with the young princess and her appeal, that the letter was shown and handed about; a copy found its way to the English court and to the Princess of Wales, by whom it was shown to the king, who was greatly struck by it'.

It has now to be clearly emphasised that the preceding material was based on biographical and historical fact: what follows now is purely conjectural, but wholly logical, and, in the absence of positive identification, it is perfectly feasible that Thomas Heming, the Court Goldsmith to the Royal Household, should wish to please his Royal Mistress by reviving happy memories for her of her own 'little victory' over Frederick the Great. It is even conceivable that the Queen herself commissioned the subject of the plaque, namely, a group portrait of Frederick the Great and his officers at the scene of one of his many victories in the 'Seven Years War'. One of the foremost German-Polish painters of the time, Daniel Nicholas Chodowiecki (1726–1801), who painted Frederick many times might have executed the original painting from which Heming drew inspiration.

It is indeed a far cry from an unidentified portrait plaque on a silver casket to a detailed and unusually inspiring vignette in the life of a beloved monarch. To the devoted researcher, however, this linking of fact and history with fiction and conjecture is part of the absorbing nature of his work: the most fascinating aspect of this, is that an inanimate object can also, on occasion, 'tell its own story'

3. Applied Orna- ment

In order to facilitate a more complete understanding of the techniques involved in 'Applied Ornament', namely, most of the categories of enrichment which appear on silver boxes, it becomes necessary to introduce a new concept which, through its very simplicity, appears to have been overlooked by earlier pioneers in this subject, and which, after some clarification, could open new vistas to the student. It will therefore be of some benefit to indulge in a comparative survey, although, at first glance, this does not appear to have any connection with the matter under discussion.

The simple truth is that it has not been generally realised that 'ornament' is a much subtler device than it appears to be: it is not only an enrichment, designed to cover bare surfaces or hide imperfections, it is also the silversmith's answer to the painter's art of *chiaroscuro*, literally, 'light and shade', the device attributed to Leonardo da Vinci which provides depth and perspective to an otherwise flat surface, in other words, the much coveted 'Third Dimension'. Thus a box enriched with 'ornament' not only possesses absorbing embellishment, but imparts a feeling of spaciousness and continuity; it is as if, were it possible, the owner could 'step inside' the frame of the lid and share the experiences of the figures or subjects placed therein.

It may well be that Leonardo initiated the trend, but earlier examples, if the more crudely applied, remain extant to show that man has long been preoccupied with the craft of perspective; a plate in the Hermitage Museum at Leningrad, made *circa* A.D. 527–567 in the reign of the Emperor Justinian I, illustrates early Byzantine trends towards perspective. The relief is not high, but the impression of depth is achieved by the positions of the various figures portrayed. The subject is 'A shepherd with his flock', and a goat appears to be nibbling the branches of a tree in the far background (actually the top left of the picture), while another goat is centrally placed, to the right of the main subject, and a dog with its paw raised, is in the extreme foreground. These devices have the effect of placing the shepherd in the centre of the composition, which is, in fact, on a perfectly plain surface.

Following Leonardo's invention (it could well have been merely a revival, as many art-forms were lost during the 'Dark Ages' to reappear with the Renaissance) it is significant that the use of perspective appears on plate (as well as in paintings) from the third quarter of the 16th century. Two forms were employed: cast and engraved ornament, and both seem to have been parallel with each other, but whereas the former technique was used by the Swiss and German silversmiths, who were particularly skilled in its application, the latter belonged mainly to the Netherlands, primarily Holland.

The great Nuremberg craftsman, Christoph Jamnitzer (1563–1618) was a master of perspective in silver. His famous series of 'Phaeton Kredentzschalen', that is, standing dishes made partly for show but also for offering wine to an honoured guest, are splendid manifestations of his craft. They are illustrated in Rosenberg's *Der Goldschmiede Merkzeichen*, plates 84-5. One of the tazzae depicts the sisters of Phaeton, son of Helios, (who was slain by Zeus for driving the chariot of the sun to earth, thus endangering the world) bewailing his death. In keeping with the mythological legend, which states that they were turned into poplar trees for doing so, the figures sprout leaves and branches from their heads; two of the figures are in front of, and two behind, a magnificently sculptured sarcophagus, which is shown in full perspective, thus achieving a bewildering effect of 'depth'.

The German engravers, too, produced beautiful perspective effects, and one, the Liège born, German domiciled artist Johann Theodor de Bry (1561–1623) was able to refine the process even further by the use of a yet simpler device: he also produced a series of standing dishes, of much the same form as Jamnitzer's 'Kredentzschalen', except that his tazzae were of deeper concave form, so that the outside figures in the engraving appeared to look inward towards the centrally placed figures. The effect was further heightened by the introduction of architecture at either side of the composition and in the background, creating the illusion of *chiaroscuro* yet once again. The eminent contemporary specialist on ornament, John F. Hayward, wrote an important article on this subject for *Apollo Miscellany* in 1950.

Several series of engraved dessert and dinner plates of English provenance but by foreign artists are extant: these include the two sets, dated 1567 and 1569 engraved by Pieter Maas of Cologne. The latter illustrates the story of the Prodigal Son, and the former (a set of twelve) 'The Labours of Hercules'. Again, by the use of architecture and masonry, an illusion of perspective has been created. The famous 'Strawberry Hill Sale' of the effects of **Horace** Walpole, held in April, 1842, contained a set of twelve dessert plates engraved by Simon van de Passe comprising the story of the Prodigal Son. The date was not given in the catalogue.

So much for engraved ornament which sets out to create a deliberate illusion of perspective. The ornamentation of silver boxes was often so cunningly effected that the owner was quite unaware of the deception which was being practiced upon him, while at the same time he experienced a feeling of well-being on beholding the box. For, and there seems little doubt about it, people like boxes for their own sake, not for the purpose or the contents. Where the article is quite unadorned, the simplicity of 'line' or the 'feel' of the patination satisfy the senses, but where there is clever enrichment, this gratification can be overwhelming.

A fleeting review of some of the methods embodying *chiaroscuro* of one kind or another may serve to emphasise this point: casting and engraving having been already summarily dealt with (they are examined at greater length later in this chapter) there remain other media where most subtle use of the device may be observed. Of these, 'piqué-work', which was popular in the late 17th-early 18th centuries is a good example. Three superb specimens in the medium are illustrated. Basically, the technique consisted of a tortoiseshell or mother-of-pearl ground inlaid with silver patterns or motifs. Examine the top specimen which depicts a 'Breughelesque' group engaged in some sort of dance, but which is actually the traditional English Morris Dance, with all ten figures appearing. Nine figures link hands in an apparent 'circle', and the feeling of depth here, is most realistically achieved by placing the inlay in an ellipse, with the figure of the bag-piper in the centre, thus, the figures in the foreground appear entirely separate from those in the back. The costumes are traditional and there are plumes of mother-of-pearl in their hats. One of the characters (at bottom left) seems to have his leg supported in a mother-of-pearl crutch. The 'stomping' back-view of the figure at top centre is a most beautifully judged vignette of a peasant at play. This particular box was part of the famous Berney Collection of Piqué, and was sold in June, 1927, when it was ascribed in the catalogue to the 17th century and as of English origin.

William III oval tobacco box: with 'stand-away' hinge of the five-lugged variety. The 'stepped' lid superbly engraved with contemporary 'smoking and drinking' scene, symbolic of 'the good life', depicting a lighted octagonal candlestick or taperstick enriched with its own Coat-of-Arms, two crossed churchwarden pipes on a paper containing tobacco, a baluster wine glass and a straw-bound wine bottle, on a finely engraved pedestal table. Overall flies a bird, holding a motto ribbon in its beak which bears the Latin motto: 'Ne Quid Nimis' or 'Nothing in Excess'.
Maker's mark obscured, London 1700.
Size: 4 inches by 3½ inches by 1 inch deep.

William IV shallow oval snuffbox: the lid with 'stand-away' hinge and enriched with repoussé *chiaroscuro* subject: A 'Tavern Scene' in the manner of Teniers the Younger.
Maker: John B. Caw, Edinburgh 1831.
Size: 3 inches by 2⅜ inches by ½ an inch deep.
This box is fully discussed and analysed in the text.

Further examples of perspective in ornament may be observed in many of the boxes illustrated: these include the marvellously conceived 'Jacobite Relic', which depicts Charles I descending from Heaven; here, the domed lid lends depth to the subject. It is, in fact, the very antithesis of the German 'Kredenzschalen', in that it is of convex form, whereas the latter are concave, but the effect is almost the same. The chequered foreground extends to the very rim of the box, and thus serves effectively to create a 'natural horizon', or the dividing line between the ground and the sky, so that the countryside with the rolling hills and church-spires, houses and trees recede into the background. Of course, the medium which so beautifully achieves this separation is the centrally placed table which appears to be hexagonal in shape: the major portion of this protrudes into the foreground, thereby increasing the perspective.

Another superbly engraved 'depth picture' may be found on the oval hinged William III Tobacco Box dated London 1700. Here, the engraver chose a 'still-life' subject of a rectangular table upon which are various symbols of 'the good life': twin pipes crossed over a twist of tobacco, a lighted octagonal taper-stick complete with an engraved Coat-of-Arms on the base, a wine-bottle bound in straw, and to provide the *chiaroscuro* effect, a baluster wine-glass placed in front

Charles II 'pique-inlay' snuffbox: the tortoise-shell ground delightfully inlaid with 'Breughelesque' motifs—a group of ten peasants dancing the 'Morris Dance', one of whom is a bagpiper— in silver and mother-of-pearl inlay. The whole contained in a 'debased laurel' frame, also of silver.
Unmarked, *circa* 1680-90.
This box, which is discussed in both the chapter on 'Applied Ornament' and the section on 'pique-inlay'. was sold in the Berney Sale of Pique-work at Sotheby's, on the 22nd of June, 1927, where it was described as being of the 'pique-posé' variety, that is, the pattern was pressed into a pattern previously embossed.
Size: 3⅞ inches by 2½ inches.

of one of the churchwarden pipes. An extremely interesting feature of this engraver's skill, which could so easily be missed, ought to be especially noted: on the 'flat heel' of the bowl of the pipe inclining towards the left, he has placed the initials 'T.K.' Now, a very careful perusal of Adrian Oswald's monumental analysis of *English Clay Tobacco Pipes*, reprinted by the British Archaeological Association from their 1960 Journal (third series Vol. XXIII) reveals that although this painstaking researcher lists more than 10,000 clay pipe-makers, not one 'T.K' appears. It would therefore be apparent that these are the owner's own initials, yet another little sly touch to please, and it may well be that if properly analysed, the Coat-of-Arms on the taperstick would yield the identity of the family to whom it originally belonged.

The various devices to which the craftsmen turned to satisfy their passion for perspective gradually developed into a fascinating medium for study in its own right: the 'repoussé-top' boxes will shortly be discussed in some detail, but one outstanding specimen deserves to be singled out for special mention. Quite apart from its other merits, it is the only Scottish box appearing in this work (it was felt that the inclusion of one solitary Scots specimen did not warrant a change of title to 'British Silver Boxes') and, in addition, it, too, possesses this sense of a 'picture in the round'.

The subject is a 'Topers' Scene' in the manner of Teniers, and the device of *chiaroscuro* is here divided between the rectangular bench which one figure bestraddles and the centrally placed circular table around which the card-players sit. The angle at which the bench is placed serves to emphasise the depth of the room. The lusty players (one has obviously been dealt a 'bad hand') engage their feet beneath the circular table, and yet again, a feeling of perspective has been attained.

It was presumably inevitable that the passion for 'Baroque-type' extravaganza

William III 'pique-inlay' snuffbox: of oval shape, with 'stand-away' hinge pinned to lid. The lid superlatively inlaid with silver foliate motifs in an ellipse and an inner cartouche of similar type. Tortoishell ground and base. The hinge of the 11-lugged variety. Unmarked, *circa* 1700.
Size: 3½ inches by 2¼ inches by ½ an inch deep.

George II 'pique-inlay' snuffbox: of oval form, the lid enriched with 'masks and arabesques' motifs and two parrots pulling at a basket of flowers. The inner scrolling cartouche lends form and shape to the outer foliate scrolls. Unmarked *circa* 1730.
Size: 3 inches by 2¼ inches.
The mask at the top of the cartouche is in pure Pompeiian style, but the parrots are of French taste of the period of Louis XV. It is probable, however, that this box is of English origin, being influenced by the French designs in the same manner as the silver of the Huguenot craftsman was in the late 17th and early 18th centuries.

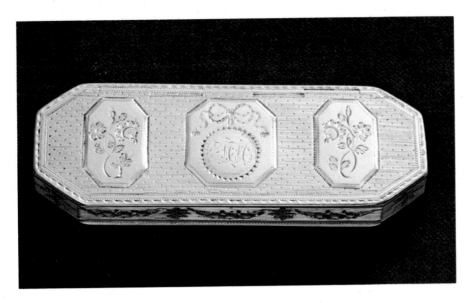

George III rectangular cut-corner toothpick case: superbly bright-cut with three octagonal panels containing floral sprays and a contemporary monogram in a festooned escutcheon on a 'double-dot' scored ground. With fine 'hidden-integral' hinge, the sides enriched with swags of foliate bright-cutting.
Makers: Phipps and Robinson, London 1789.
Size: 3⅛ inches by 1 inch by ¼ of an inch deep.

which assailed Europe during the 18th century should spread to enrichment on boxes, and many fine specimens of this trend remain extant, but more curiously, there was an apparent revival of these themes in England in the second decade of the 19th century, and Birmingham craftsmen in particular, Joseph Taylor and John Barber are but two, worked in this medium. Seeking about for suitable subjects where 'depth' existed, they settled on a series of mythological subjects, and, from very careful research, which has failed to locate the exact sources of their *genre*, it would seem that the casters and modellers created an amalgam of themes. Thus, in analysing the superb silver-gilt snuffbox by Taylor dated 1821, it is possible to discern the subject as 'Aeneas fleeing from Troy with his father Anchises who carries the household gods (or Penates)', but quite impossible to locate the source. Of course, it is possible that the actual painting does exist, but an examination of A. Pigler's *Barockthemen*, published in Budapest 1956, which lists thousands of paintings, reveals that it could be from Tintoretto's school, or from the hand of twenty other artists, or from none, and where does the search begin?

The feeling of perspective in this case is created by two illusions: the heavy scrolling 'baroque border' and the receding figures of soldiery in the background, a splendidly-prowed rowing boat at bottom left, from which the central figure, presumably Aeneas, is stepping, and a fallen column to Aeneas' right, but in the very centre of the group. There is a turreted and castellated castle in the far background.

Not quite so subtle, perhaps, but still possessing a certain 'depth', is the group which can be easily identified as 'Diogenes' dialogue with Alexander the Great'. It will be recalled that the king, on asking which boon the great Greek philosopher and cynic would most crave, received the reply that his desire was that 'the king would not stand between him and the sun!' The illusion of perspective is

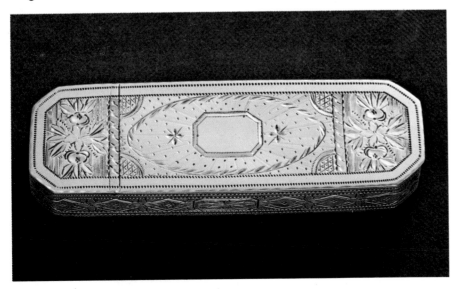

George III finely bright-cut rectangular cut-corner toothpick case: the lid with 'raying bright-cut' enrichment and octagonal rectangular escutcheon in centre for monogram, and foliate bright-cut motifs at either end of the lid, and formed as 'diapers' on sides. With finely constructed 'hidden-integral' hinge. With velvet lining and mirror inside lid.
Maker: Samuel Pemberton **vi**, Birmingham 1791.
Size: 3⅛ inches by 1 inch by ¼ of an inch deep.

Bright-Cutting

here achieved by placing the famous 'tub' in which Diogenes is said to have lived, amidst a mass of trees and foliage, so that the figure of Diogenes appears to 'stand out'. Furthermore, the latter's arm, pointing towards the king, obscures the uniform of the soldier in the centre, thus creating an 'artificial horizon'. The figure of Alexander, to the right, is, in turn, emphasised by placing it in front of the group of warriors in the background.

Yet once again, it has not been possible to trace the source of this subject, but it might have been executed by any painter of the Classical Period, and could have been taken directly from a contemporary engraving, of the same period as the box. The English engraver Richard Earlom (1742–1822) was particularly active in these historical and mythological themes.

A most surprising medium for *chiaroscuro*, and one which would seem most unsuited to the illusion, is the technique of bright-cutting. A brief definition of the method can be of service here: it is 'engraving in free style, without the limitations of 'drawing in' the pattern'. This requires elaboration: in most other types of engraving, the artist either worked from imagination (as on many later Birmingham-made boxes, where contemporary trends in fashion and commerce were mirrored, without recourse to pre-conceived designs, with a few notable

George III rectangular snuffbox: the lid beautifully bright-cut with 'diaper' motifs and the centre rectangular panel containing elliptical 'cross hatching' on a 'double-dot' scored ground. The sides similarly enriched, and with contemporary monograms in oval escutcheons on lid and side.
Makers: Phipps and Robinson, London 1798.
Size: 2¾ inches by 2½ inches by ¾ of an inch deep.

George III rectangular cut-corner snuffbox: the surfaces superlatively bright-cut with foliate sprays and swags on 'scored threaded' ground, and with 'fans' and 'musical theme' motif on lid. With finely constructed 'hidden-integral' hinge.
Makers: Phipps and Robinson, London 1791.
Size: 3 inches by 2½ inches by ¾ of an inch deep.

exceptions) or traced the motif on a gamboge-coating, that is, a yellow resinous substance which darkened the surface of the silver and thus facilitated the engraving. In 'bright-cutting', the engraver used specially prepared tools, primarily the 'square graver'—a type of 'scorper' or 'scooper'—which were kept in a state of sharpness by an emery-stick, and by placing the full weight of his body behind every 'cut', produced the effect of 'depth'.

This very special technique appears to have arisen in the mid-1760's, although specimens of this very early period are very rare. It involved (and still does, but for very few craftsmen, as the art of bright-cutting by hand is a dying craft) absolute confidence on the part of the engraver. Working, with very few exceptions (these being the famous 'Adam Motifs') entirely 'freehand', he proceeded to build up the feeling of perspective by a series of different devices. The 'ground', that is, the actual surface of the metal was 'scored in' by the 'threading-tool', giving, as the term implies, a series of thin parallel lines. Even this conventional background was made to appear deeper by lighter and heavier strokes, giving the effect, yet again, of *chiaroscuro*. The illusion was further accentuated by 'optical deception', namely, slanting lines working away from the central motif, which might be a floral or foliate design or a manteled cartouche containing a

Coat-of-Arms. The centrally placed design thus attained a 'three-dimensional' appearance.

A favourite method used by London bright-cutters (the Phipps and Robinson partnership was particularly successful in this medium) was to employ a 'double-dot' scorper, that is, a tool with a cutting-face so incised, and engrave an ellipse which seemed to consist of hundreds of 'dots'. It was actually a type of 'cross-hatching', namely, engraving in parallel lines in two series, crossing each other, and using 'straights and curves'. The design was then further enriched by a centrally placed cartouche and the effect was complete. For brevity's sake, this effect is often known as 'raying bright-cut' ornament.

The 'double-dot' method was also employed in 'diaper' or 'diamond-shape' designs, and the 'threading-tool' was used to engrave the outside 'lozenge' or to provide a 'ground' for the foliage. Nowhere is the use of 'thread' motifs so successfully illustrated as on the superb rectangular snuffbox bearing a gold portrait bust of George III. The bust is also cast in relief, so that the figure appears to emerge from the very centre of the lid.

It must be emphasised that the 'wear and tear' of centuries, that is, the patination, has contributed to the charm of bright-cutting, as a piece of new plate with newly applied ornament (in spite of polishing) was quite rough to the touch. It is recalled with amusement that a perfectly genuine George III tea-tray was condemned by several 'specialists' as 'modern engraving', because the bright-cutting was sharp to the touch. Of course, in that particular case, the explanation was quite simple: the article was in absolutely 'brilliant state', and the engraving had never been polished! On close examination, under a glass, the process, like so many others, becomes nonsensical: it appears to consist, as on a pair of sugar-tongs, for instance, of a series of 'nicks and wriggles'; it is only when the object is viewed in perspective that the effect is realised to be 'light and shade'.

Finally, before passing to other methods of 'illusion', it is necessary to examine a very common motif which appears on many articles of English plate from the early 17th century: the 'Acanthus-leaf' design. Of course, the very name is derived from the Greek, in which language it is the term for 'spike', which is as good a description as any for its elegant but spiky leaves. The best-known species today is *Acanthus mollis* (bear's breech), but the ancients favoured *Acanthus spinosus*, which had more finely divided leaves, and stylised the natural plant into an elegant art-form. As an enrichment on silver it is particularly effective because the leaves are deeply incised and 'spiky-edged' to make them 'project' into the foreground, attaining once again a feeling of 'dimension'. Jackson's *History of English Plate*, in the introduction to Chapter VIII (page 204) mentions the use of acanthus foliage as an ornamental design on Elizabethan plate, but, of course, the motif is seen at its best on Roman Corinthian Capitals in ornament on architecture. Owen Jones' great work *The Grammar of Ornament*, published and superlatively illustrated in colour in 1856, devotes a chapter to this form of enrichment, but Jones believed the motif, used by the Romans as 'a scroll within a scroll' to be ineffective until 'the principle of one leaf growing out of another in a continuous line was abandoned for the adoption of a continuous stem throwing off ornaments on either side', in other words, the spreading of the motif lent perspective to the whole.

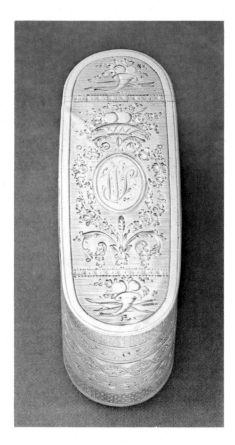

George III deep vertical oval snuffbox: enriched all over the lid (which has a 'hidden-integral' hinge) with bright-cut floral and cornucopia motifs on a·'scored threaded ground', and on the side with alternating bands of 'double-dot' scoring, foliate scrolls, and 'guilloche', that is, interlacing bands, with 'quatrefoils' in the centre. Engraved in the centre of the lid with a contemporary monogram and with a 'basket of fruit' surmounting this.
Makers: Phipps and Robinson, London 1813.
Size: 3½ inches by 1¼ inches by 2½ inches deep.

George III oval elliptical snuffbox: with a superlative 'slant-integral' hinge set in the centre of the twin lids which open at right-angles to each other. Most beautifully bright-cut with 'diaper and quatrefoil' motifs on a 'scored threaded' ground on the lids, and with similar enrichment on the side.
Makers: Phipps and Robinson, London 1787.
Size: 3 inches by 2¼ inches by ¾ of an inch deep.

George III rectangular snuffbox: engraved with 'scale-motif bright-cutting', and contemporary inscription 'Artic Regions' (the subject is not known, but it could possibly refer to a race-horse).
Makers: William Wardell and Peter Kempston, Birmingham, 1817.
The tenon and mortise hinge is shown on page 22
By Courtesy of the Birmingham Assay Office.

George III silver-gilt circular patchbox: bright-cut with foliate motifs and oval cartouche containing contemporary monogram. Bright-cut around bezel with foliate motif.
Maker: Joseph Taylor, Birmingham 1798.
Fully marked inside base, makers' mark only lid.
Size: 1⅝ inches in diameter by ½ an inch deep.

George III rectangular cut-corner snuffbox: engraved with 'raying bright-cut' enrichment in the centre of the lid, and with a superbly masked 'sunken-integral' hinge, and foliate bright-cut ornament around the rim.
Maker: Samuel Pemberton **vi**, Birmingham 1788.
This is an early specimen of bright-cutting.
Courtesy of the Birmingham Assay Office.

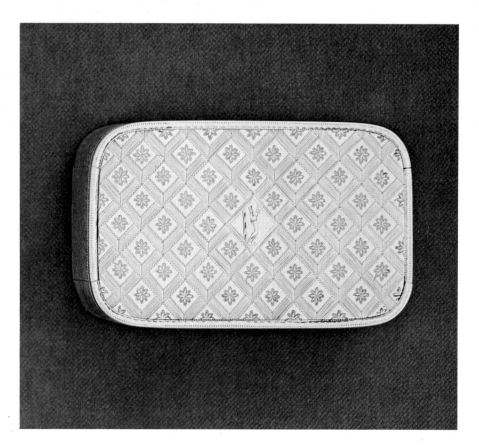

George III 'trick' snuffbox: rectangular with rounded corners. Superbly bright-cut with 'diaper and foliate' motifs and engraved in the centre diaper with contemporary 'Greyhound' crest. The 'opening mechanism' exactly matches the later William IV specimen by Edward Edwards.
Makers: Phipps & Robinson, London, 1806.
Size: 3 inches by 2½ inches.

In all, there are nine distinct methods of 'Applied Ornament' as used on silver boxes. Of these, one—bright-cutting—has already been examined; the other eight are, in order of chronology, as follows:

1. Casting.
2. Engraving.
3. Hand-carving.
4. Piqué-Inlay.
5. Engine-turning.

Methods of Enrich-ment

George III silver-gilt egg-shaped vinaigrette: possessing the finest bright-cut embellishment possible. The ovoid lid with finely concealed 'integral' hinge. The engraver first gilt the box, then bright-cut the floral and geometric motifs, and finally scored the background with the 'threading tool'. The apex of the lid bright-cut with 'snowdrop' motif. The grille is a simply pierced lift-out specimen.
Maker: Samuel Massey, London, circa 1790. (Maker's Mark only).
Size: 1½ inches by 1⅝ inches in diameter.

6. Repoussé and Embossing (allied).
7. Die-stamping.
8. Acid-etching.

It should be explained that the last two methods have been the subject of intensive research and were not previously identified with boxlid enrichment, not, that is to say, by the general public, although certain sections of the Trade might have known of their existence. In order that all these categories should be clearly understood, a short resume of *all* the techniques involved is appended, but the full research material is revealed in dealing with the latter methods.

It must be emphasised that the revelation that such important makers as Nathaniel Mills, Matthew Linwood and Joseph Willmore resorted to 'mechanical methods' in their enrichment, does not in itself indicate either impatience or contempt for the medium, but merely echoes the contemporary trend for competitive trading; there could be a vast difference between the price which a London shopkeeper might ask for a richly engraved snuffbox, and the price which he would be prepared to pay to the manufacturer. It is surely to the credit of these craftsmen that their articles lost nothing of their beauty, and actually gained some, in spite of this early form of 'mass-production'.

1. Casting

This is one of the oldest of all methods of enrichment on metalwork; all the Classical sources used it: the Greeks, the Romans and the Egyptians. Basically, the method has remained unchanged for thousands of years. Even in Egyptian Dynastic times, the *cire perdue*, that is, the 'lost-wax' method was used and was still in use when the 17th, 18th and 19th century boxes were made. Both the monk Theophilus, who wrote his famous treatise on metalworking, *Diversarum Artium Schedula* in the 12th century, and Benvenuto Cellini, the great Florentine artist of the 16th century in his *Trattato della Scultura*, described the process in detail.

Cellini's is the more concise, and is devoted to a description of the method of casting a statue. With the use of a little imagination, however, the process is much the same as that employed in casting 'plaquettes' or box-lids, and although it is somewhat lengthy in context, the description is well worth repetition, as it is still valid today. In order to cut unnecessary detail, only an abstract is given.

Cellini's Method

The figure was first modelled in clay over which a coating of wax was laid; a mixture of pounded clay, ashes and brick was then applied, till a second skin formed over the wax. Soft clay was then laid on to strengthen the mould, and the whole was thoroughly dried and placed in a hot oven, which baked the clay, both the core and the outside mould, and melted the wax which ran out from small holes made for the purpose (hence, the term 'lost-wax'). A hollow was then left, corresponding to the skin of the wax between the core and the mould, the various relations of which were preserved by various small rods of bronze which had been previously driven through from the outer mould to the rough core (in order to prevent the model from slipping). The mould was now ready, and the molten bronze was poured in till the whole space between the core and the outer mould was full. After slowly cooling, the outer mould was broken away from outside the statue and the inner core as much as possible broken up and raked out through a hole in the foot. The projecting rods of bronze were then cut away, and the whole finished by rubbing down and polishing over any roughness or defective places.

On the cast 'plaquettes' intended for boxlid enrichment, the surface was afterwards 'touched up' by hand to remove any traces of the mould, and to give further depth to the subject. This 'finishing off' process also disguised the method of manufacture. Many cast boxes have similar enrichment on the sides and on the base. These were cast in sections and later soldered together, and the inside and outside of the receptacles were then covered by fire-gilding to cover all traces of the solder-marks, as well as, of course, to protect the inside from corrosion by the acidity of the snuff or the aromatic vinegar. There are nevertheless many ungilt boxes extant, but it must be admitted that silver-gilding tends to 'heighten' the effect of *chiaroscuro*.

Fire-Gilding

Since this term is inevitably encountered in references to 'Applied Ornament', a description and definition of the process might, at this point, prove of interest. Technically speaking, the method involved the application of an *amalgam*, that is to say, a mass of gold formed into a pulp by chemical manipulation with mercury. Frederick Bradbury's important work on *A History of Old Sheffield Plate* clearly defines the process, but since it is, of course, intended for use on copper, the distinction has to be made between precious metals and base metals, otherwise, the method is basically the same.

'An amalgam was made by boiling the gold in about five times its weight of mercury in an iron ladle which had been coated with whitening and water and then dried. The amalgam, having been poured into cold water and brought to a semi-fluid condition, was put into a leather bag and squeezed to get rid of the mercury. This operation forced the mercury through the pores of the leather and left the gold in the bag. The proper consistency of the gold was about that of stiff clay, and it was divided into portions sufficient to cover the article which it was designed to gild . . . (there follows a recipe for application on copper where another amalgam of nitrate of mercury was involved) . . . then the vessels with the gold side up were placed in open pans and set over a coke fire, the heat of which caused the mercury to evaporate and leave the gold only. This process was known as fire-gilding, and is practically the same as that described in Benvenuto Cellini's treatise on Goldsmithing'. (It is interesting that Bradbury, too, made use of the same sort of comparative analysis as in the present work).

2. Engraving

This subject has already been investigated *inter alia* in relation to the work of the German, Dutch and English silversmiths, but since the method has to be included in any attempt at complete classification, a definition and historical survey is indicated.

Sir Charles Jackson's definition of 'engraving' is concise and will do as well as any, especially as he also firstly defines 'flat-chasing' (*vide: Illustrated History of English Plate*, page 208): 'It [flat-chasing] consists of surface decoration, composed of flat lines incised, or rather, depressed, with a mallet and chisel without a cutting-edge; and differs from engraving, in that the latter is executed with a sharp-edge graver which, in being used, actually cuts away a part of the metal worked upon'. The early use of engraving in England appears to stem from the 12th and 13th centuries, and, as always with very early plate, can be seen to best advantage on church silver. Both chalices and patens of these periods survive which bear simple 'Gothic' foliate ornament or the 'Agnus Dei' motif. On Tudor and Elizabethan plate, engraved ornament became more elaborate and consisted mainly of foliate scrolls in the Renaissance manner, with a leaning towards grotesque monsters and birds.

Much material has been sifted by various writers, not least by the author of this present work, in attempts to determine provenance of various articles with such eminent engravers as Simon Gribelin, William Hogarth and a few others, with little or no results, beyond conjecture. It might, therefore, be of interest, at this point, to introduce another aspect connected with 'Applied Ornament' on boxes which could supply a possible key to the identity of some of the later engravers, and which is based on critical observation and research.

With the possible exception of Fabergé (who instituted the 'workmasters' punch, and thus identified them) and some of the latter day artist-goldsmiths, whose practice of insisting that their engravers' signature appears on finely enriched plate ensures that *their* identity will be remembered, few of the work-shops of the preceding centuries subscribed to the belief that the craftsmanship of individual workers should be thus recognised. The same has, perhaps, always been true of most firms: enrichment, like most other fine work, has been taken too much for granted. It is only when it is realised that such anomalies will hamper the historian in years to come, that steps may be taken to avoid them.

In researching for possible sources of the engraved subjects on silver boxes of the late 18th and early 19th centuries, it was inevitable that the name of Thomas Bewick (1753-1828) should make an appearance. This great master-engraver lived and worked on Tyneside, and in comparing most snuffboxes and vinai-grettes of these periods, particularly of Birmingham origin, a certain 'Bewickian' atmosphere was noted about many of them. As most of Bewick's subjects were taken either from nature—his *History of Quadrupeds* and the *History of British Birds* are masterpieces in the art of the woodcut—or from contemporary life, many of the engraved scenes on the boxlids resemble these. Furthermore, Bewick had, in addition to his brother, John, a number of first-rate pupils, and altogether this 'School' turned out many thousands of superb 'cuts' or wood-cut engravings.

As has been the case, however, with the majority of the scenes noted, only a very few are directly ascribable to Bewick: the others, while in the idiom of this artist, were obviously either blatantly plagiarised, or else drew inspiration from his themes. Such few scenes as were identifiable were the Matthew Linwood subject (illustrated on page 113 of *Investing in Silver*) 'The man and his dog' (the

George IV rectangular snuff box: the sides and base engine-turned with 'basketweave' motifs and with cast foliate borders. The lid cast with mythological representation of the story of Aeneas, taken from Vergil's *Aeneid*: Aeneas fleeing from the flames of Troy, with his father, Anchises, who holds the household gods (the Penates) and leads his boy Ascanius. The whole set in a scrolling baroque frame. Maker: Joseph Taylor, Birmingham 1821.
Size: 3½ inches by 2¾ inches by ⅞ of an inch. This box is fully analysed and discussed in the text.

George III cartouche-shaped snuff box: silver-gilt, the lid with cast 'Topers' Scene' in the manner of Teniers the Younger or Ostade. Of superb quality and in the finest *chiaroscuro* effect.
Makers: T. J. and N. Creswick, Sheffield 1812.
Size: 4 inches by 3 inches by ⅞ of an inch deep. This box is engraved on the base with the following inscription: 'James Creswick, Crookes Moor, Sheffield'. This, therefore, is the maker's own snuff box, and is suitably magnificent; it is in absolutely mint condition.

George IV rectangular oval snuff box: the lid of the oval 'flap' variety placed in the centre of the top surface, and has a florally enriched cast border and a 'hidden-integral' hinge. The enrichment takes the form of 'eccentric engine-turning', by means of which a 'Gothic' effect is attained.
Maker: Joseph Willmore, Birmingham 1820.
Size: 3½ inches by 2½ inches by 1 inch deep.

dog watches while his master is having his dinner) stated by Thomas Hugo in his *The Bewick Collector*, London, 1866, to appear as a tail-piece in the first edition of *British Quadrupeds*, and the Pemberton 'Hare in the reeds', a cast version of which by Thomas Newbold also appears within these pages.

One concrete conclusion which emerged from a close examination of all the thousands of Bewick woodcuts in the British Museum was the fact that both he and some of his pupils also engraved trade cards, letter-headings and invoice heads for various Newcastle personalities. Bewick himself engraved the silver-smith John Robertson's trade card in 1814, and, as he is known to have engraved at least one salver (it is now in the Victoria and Albert Museum) and had been first the apprentice and then the partner of Ralph Beilby, who was a gifted engraver on silver, it is possible that he produced work for other silversmiths also, possibly John Robertson.

Taking this coincidence as a possible key to the identity of other copper-plate engravers who might have worked in silver, the Birmingham Trade Directories were perused, and a few more names isolated:

1). FRANCIS EGINTON, *circa* 1800, who engraved Joseph Taylor's trade card and also that of Taylor & Perry (the artist who worked for the latter might

George III silver-gilt cast-top snuffbox: the lid cast with baroque scrolling motif and 'Fortuna or Ceres in her Temple, holding a cornucopia'. With vine motifs on the sides. Maker: Matthew Linwood **v**, Birmingham 1816.
Courtesy of the Birmingham Assay Office.

George IV snuffbox: with cast lid. Subject: Diogenes' dialogue with Alexander the Great (This subject is analysed in the text).
Maker: Thomas Shaw, Birmingham, 1825.
Courtesy of the Birmingham Assay Office.

This maker is sometimes confused with Thomas Spicer, but, in fact, Spicer was a watch-case maker, who did not make vinaig-rettes or snuffboxes. He worked between 1816-42.

have been a son of the former, with the same Christian name, as the card was necessarily later: Taylor & Perry did not enter their mark until 1829).

2). THE TYE FAMILY, *circa* 1815-30. These were all associated in some manner with silversmithing: Edward Tye was a gilt-toy (probably silverware) and pearl-bead manufacturer, George Tye and William Postans (better known as Postans & Tye) made the charming little 'engraved scene' snuffbox which depicts University College, Oxford in 1823, and the conclusion that the scene was engraved by yet another Tye—John—who worked as an engraver and copperplate printer at 12 Cherry Street, becomes irresistible, especially in view of the fact that he also engraved an advertisement for T. Hampton, Gun and Pistol Manufacturer of Livery Street, which shows the usual mid-1820-30 'Hunting Scene' subject, with mounted huntsmen, pointers and countryside motifs.

3). JOHN REYNOLDS, *circa* 1800-30, who engraved Samuel Pemberton's advertisements.

4). THOMAS COCKS, *circa* 1805-30, who appeared in the Birmingham Trade Directories as an engraver and copperplate printer. The fact that his name is spelled thus and not 'Cox' would appear to limit the possibility that he was not the partner of John Bettridge, who was also active at about this time. This would explain the excellence of this partnership's work, namely, the fact that for once, work did not have to be sent to an 'outworker' but that the engraver worked on the premises, thus permitting a far closer relationship between maker and engraver, who could consult each other on various important points arising. Bettridge's mark is often confused with that of John Barber, who produced most of the finer small articles bearing the 'J.B.' mark, and is accordingly credited as such in this work.

George III large rectangular snuffbox: the lid engraved with 'raying bright-cut' enrichment, and embellished with applique bust of George III in gold. The border engraved with 'double-dot' scoring. The hinge is of the 'sunken-integral' type. With scalloped thumbpiece.
Maker: Joseph Willmore, Birmingham, 1817. Engraved with the following presentation inscription:
'A Token of Respect from the Noncommissioned Officers and Privates of the Holne Pierrepoint Troup of Volunteer Cavelry To Capt Bettison, August 12th, 1817'.
Courtesy of the Birmingham Assay Office.

67

This group includes all the 'allied materials', namely, treen, and its sub-divisions, natural products—ivory, mother-of-pearl, tortoiseshell (both the opaque type and thinly sliced finely figured), cameos, striated and moss agate, aventurine, and semi-precious stones such as cornelian—and man-made patterns such as mosaics.

The divisions of treen are as follows:

Boxwood: this wood possesses a smooth texture which commended itself as a natural medium for hand-carving, and many fine religious items as well as secular articles were both carved and engraved. A mid-19th century definition is specific: 'Box is a very valuable wood. It is of a yellowish colour, close grained, very hard and heavy'. Certainly, the silver-mounted specimen illustrated is an excellent example of its versatility.

Walnut: this is an uncommon wood in use for snuffboxes, although hollowed-out walnut-bole (the gnarled sucker on the trunk of the tree) tobacco boxes of very large size have been observed, which were lead-lined and richly ornamented on the lids with armorial bearings. The walnut tree as a species is mentioned in the earliest British botanical writings and it is supposed to have been introduced by the Romans. An inventory of 1587 lists *A bedsteed of wallnuttry, in Ladies chamber.*

3. Hand-Carved Allied Materials

Treen

Large George IV rectangular snuffbox: heavily cast all over with acanthus motifs. Makers: Lawrence & Co. Birmingham, 1826. Size: 4 inches by 1¾ inches by 1¼ inches deep. *Courtesy of the Birmingham Assay Office.*

Ivory

This natural material (from the tusks of elephant, rhinoceros, walrus) has very ancient origins. The Golden Age of the ivory carver was at its height in the 13th century, but the craft went on well into the 17th. Most boxes made in this medium stem from the late 1680's, but a very finely carved-lid specimen, fully lined with silver, and thus fully hall-marked, has been noted. It was made (or at least put together) by John Leach, London, 1716.

Tortoiseshell

As may be discerned from the mid-18th century comment of Edward Holdsworth in his *Remarks and Dissertations upon Virgil*, 1746, the medium is very old: 'Some of the Romans were so extravagant as to cover their doors and door-cases [the inner lining of the doorway] with Indian Tortoiseshell'. With the advent, in the late 17th century, of the craftsman John Obrisset (for fuller details *vide Investing in Silver*, page 101) a series of moulded designs and portrait busts were pressed in this material, and some, very few, were engraved, as in the specimen illustrated.

Mother-of-Pearl

This is a by-product of certain bivalvular molluscs, primarily the *Pinna*, from which the majority of *nacre*—a smooth, shining, iridescent substance forming the inner layer of the shell—is derived. The use of mother-of-pearl in ornament on

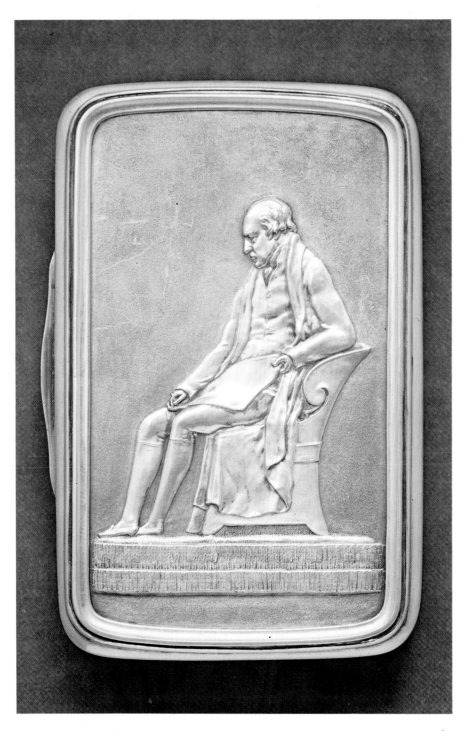

Left
Victorian 'table-size' snuffbox: of rectangular shape, silver-gilt, the border cast with National Emblems, comprising Rose, Thistle and Shamrock motifs, the centre panel engine-turned with 'basketweave' motif, and containing a cartouche bearing a contemporary monogram. The sides and base similarly engine-turned.
Maker: Edward Edwards, London, 1843.
Size: 5 inches by 4 inches by 1¾ inches deep.

Victorian cast-top snuffbox: with vertical portrait of the Watt Memorial in Handsworth Church, erected 1824, by Chantrey.
Maker: Nathaniel Mills, **ii,** Birmingham, 1838. Weight: 7 oz. 3 dwts.
(This box is fully discussed in the text).
Courtesy of the Birmingham Assay Office.

boxes is frequent, but handcarved specimens are uncommon, especially from the hands of English craftsmen—the work is more reminiscent of the next category.

A very few boxes, chiefly vinaigrettes, and, very occasionally, a snuffbox have been observed with a hand-carved cameo set in a silver frame into the lid. As most of these are of Italian origin, the subject selected for the enrichment is normally of a classical nature—the specimen illustrated depicts Venus and Cupid —finely carved. Margaret Flower in her excellent work on *Victorian Jewellery* published in 1951, states that 'The manufacture of shell cameos, the *Art Journal* of 1854 tells us, is said to be of Sicilian origin, and has been carried on at Rome since about 1805. However in about 1830 an Italian began the carving of shell cameos in Paris, "and at the present time (1854) a much larger number of shell cameos are made in Paris than in Italy. The Roman artists have attained perfection in this beautiful art".' The writer continues: 'The shells chiefly used are the red and white Bull's Mouth, the pink and white Queen's Conch, and the brown and white Black Helmet'.

The term 'agate' embraces a semi-precious stone which occurs, in the natural state, either in eruptive rocks, such as ancient lava, or in veins, as found in the

Cameos

Agate

George III rectangular oval snuffbox: the lid and sides cast overall with floral enrichment and with small 'shell' terminal and thumb-piece. The centre of the lid with inset oval portrait bust of William Shakespeare in a gold frame under glass, the sides with beaded rims.
Maker: Francis Higgins, London 1819.
Size: 3¾ inches by 2½ inches by ¾ of an inch deep.

George IV small rectangular snuffbox: silver-gilt, with cast finely modelled butterfly on lid, and projecting thumbpiece.
Maker: John Bridge, London 1825.
Size: 1¾ inches by 1 inch by ¾ of an inch deep. The exact purpose of this 'butterfly' motif is not known, but is possibly purely decorative in origin.

Right
George III silver-gilt rectangular cast-top snuffbox: subject: a tavern scene in the 'Teniers' manner', set in a scrolling foliate cartouche. The sides and base finely engine-turned with the 'basketweave' motif.
Maker: **J.F.** (not known, either to Jackson or to the Register at Goldsmiths' Hall), London, 1818.
Size: 3½ inches by 2⅜ inches by ¾ of an inch deep.

George III silver-gilt rectangular cast-top snuffbox: the lid with cast 'coursing and foxhunting' subjects, and foliate sprays at each corner. Set in centre with engine-turned panel of the 'basketweave' motif.
Maker: **DH**, London, 1813.
Size: 3¾ inches by 2½ inches.
This maker's mark is not at Goldsmiths' Hall, nor is it that of David Hennell. In his informative genealogical survey *The Hennells Identified*, published in *The Connoisseur*, December 1955, Percy Hennell said the following: 'Just when the eldest son David ceased active participation in the craft is not known, as, although he was a livery member of the Goldsmiths' Company from 1791 until he resigned in 1841, Mark 6 (the famous **RH/DH** mark in a square punch of Robert and David Hennell) is only found up to about 1804'.

George III silver-gilt cast-top snuffbox: the lid cast with 'flowerheads' on matt-chased ground: the motif is repeated on the base. With applique 'herringbone' motifs on side. No maker's mark, London, 1807.
Size: 3½ inches by 2¼ inches.

George IV silver-gilt cast-top snuffbox: subject: 'Pointer in a field'. The rim heavily cast with foliate motifs, and the sides and base with engine-turned 'basketweave' motifs. Makers: Ledsam, Vale & Wheeler, Birmingham 1828.
Size: 3¼ inches by 2¼ inches.

German region of Saxony. There were also enormous deposits of the mineral in another German district, around the town of Oberstein, and a great trading centre sprang up which produced superlative examples in this most attractive medium. At the Great Exhibition of 1851, for example, several articles made in various types of agate were exhibited, and, to quote the *Report of the Juries* (all items to be exhibited were first examined for standards of merit) 'The manufacture of articles in onyx and agate, in their natural state or coloured of various hues by artificial processes—(the art of 'staining' was mentioned by Pliny and was a closely guarded secret for centuries; primarily red staining is obtained by means of ferric oxide, blue by salt of iron and a solution of ferro-cyanide, green by salts of nickel or chromium, and yellow by hydrochloric acid)—has become a large branch of industry at Oberstein'.

When sliced in section, the mineral revealed beautiful markings; the 'moss-agate', which was always believed to arise from vegetable infiltration into the chalcedony, is in reality due to the infiltration of various oxides.

Aventurine

This is a variety of quartz containing spangles of mica or scales of iron-oxide, which lend brilliancy to the mineral. It is mostly of Russian origin, and was mined in the Ural Mountains. Mostly reddish-brown or yellow in colour, it is also found in green, but an artificial form was discovered by chance when a workman at a glassworks near Venice accidentally let some copper filings fall into the molten 'metal', and thus the name, which also means 'accident' in Italian, was originated. The blue and gold spangled variety noted on several boxlids is of this second type, namely, the artificial variety. Oddly enough, the medium was also extensively used on Old Sheffield Plate boxes of the early 1740 period, possibly in imitation of the more expensive agate panels which appeared on silver boxes.

Cornelian

This is, like agate, another variety of chalcedony, but has a deep reddish colour, and is transparent if cut thinly; it is mostly encountered as an embellishment on late 17th century spice-boxes, but early 18th century snuffboxes, too, have cornelian bosses, or knobs. In late 18th century boxes, the panels might form the sides, but this type is uncommon.

Mosaics

The widening facilities for continental travel in the 1840's and 50's, permitted souvenir-hunters to sample European art-forms, and many travellers returned to England with mosaic inlays which were then applied to boxlid ornamentation;

this, in turn, persuaded the ever-adventurous craftsmen to introduce this newly popular motif into their embellishment. It should be stated, however, that the Phipps and Robinson partnership (ever pioneering) was producing similar effects at the beginning of the 19th century, but with larger stones—the Victorian effect was obtained by the use of small multi-coloured chips set in a circle or a rectangle and outlined with further, but longer chips—and it is possible that other Georgian craftsmen also used the motif.

Various Italian views were popular subjects for mosaic inlay: scenic panoramas, the Ruins of Pompeii, The Colosseum at Rome, and groups involving domestic animals—sheep, dogs and horses—as well as specially commissioned subjects, such as favourite pets or a few portraits—have also been noted. From the historical point of view, mosaic enrichment is very ancient, and is found on Greek, Roman and Byzantine ornament. The Italian craftsmen of the mid-19th century excelled in this craft and sent several superb specimens to the Great Exhibition.

4. Piqué Inlay

This group is difficult to ascribe to any one origin, as both English and French craftsmen worked in the medium from about 1675 to 1730. The type probably originated in France (there is still some controversy over the identity of the inventor) but, as with many other art-forms, the English workers were quick to follow the fashion. As was stated above (in relation to the 'Morris Dancers' Box') the types of the figures used drew inspiration from Old Master paintings, but it is interesting to note that the third example illustrated, while it is decorated in the French manner, with 'masks and arabesques', drew *its* inspiration, not from French, but ancient Pompeiian ornament, with the exception, of course, of the parrots!

5. Engine Turning

This subject has received little or no careful study, and yet is one of the oldest techniques employed in 'Applied Ornament'. Most writers ascribe the craft to the middle of the 18th century and speak of it in passing. In fact, it is one of the most significant methods of enrichment, capable of subtle effects, and useful for more than one purpose. The main function of engine-turning, or 'Rose-engine Turning' as it ought to be designated (this is the name of the lathe on which the embellishment was done) was to provide a feeling of 'texture' to the metal, perhaps yet another form of *chiaroscuro*, but it is not generally realised that its secondary function was to protect the actual surface of the metal from excessive wear. The 'ridges and corrugations' resulting from the 'turning' were not

Left and right
George IV snuffbox of large size, with reeded lid and base and foliate thumbpiece. The base has cast 'self-legs', so that the box is lifted off the surface of the table.
Maker: Joseph Taylor, Birmingham 1823.
Size: 4 inches.
Courtesy of the Birmingham Assay Office.

exceptionally deeply incised, but they did provide a 'ground' which prevented loving fingers from damaging the box by continual smoothing.

The method known as 'engine-turning' is very old: probably dating from the late Renaissance, but it was not used for metalwork until the end of the 17th century; its primary use as a form of enrichment was on ivory and boxwood. The catalogue of the Franks Bequest in the British Museum illustrates an ivory tankard mounted in silver-gilt of South German provenance, dated *circa* 1680, on which the whole of the ivory portion is 'turned on the lathe in a series of horizontal bands of several designs, two of them being wavy'. An illuminating footnote informs the reader that 'Nuremberg was a fruitful centre for the production of the wildest vagaries in the art of turning on the lathe, and a number of examples are to be seen in the museum Collection of Ivories. The Zick family, father (died 1632) and sons (one died 1666) were especially famous for such *tours de force* of misplaced ingenuity'. This last information would certainly support the claim, made by a senior Birmingham craftsman (whose workshop continues to produce hand-turned silver articles of the most superlative quality) that engine-turning was 'at least three hundred and fifty years old'.

The earliest method for turning metalwork on a lathe to produce decorative patterns was probably of French origin, although this is by no means certain. Perhaps the earliest manual on the subject was written by Charles Plumier under the title *L'Art de Tourner*, and published at Lyons in 1701. The work informs the reader in its subtitle on the frontispiece that it deals not only with turning in treen and ivory, but also iron and *other metals*, and goes on to list all the geometric shapes and effects obtainable with various tools.

The earliest ornamental turning lathe traceable is in the Science Museum, London, and is dated 'late 17th century'. It is of the 'treadle' type, and beautifully preserved. The following is an abstract from the catalogue of *Machine Tools Collection* at the Museum: 'The nose end of the mandrel (the axis to which the work is secured) runs in a cylindrical collar and the pointed back end is supported in a hollowed adjustable centre. When rose-turning, the collar is released by removing a locking screw so that it is free to swing about a pivot in the headstock (the support for the revolving parts). The mandrel carries a group of ten rosettes (these are the pattern discs, so called because they resemble a floral motif), any one of which may be made to press against a rubber (the implement used for smoothing the surface of the metal) which may be fixed anywhere along a bar running parallel with the mandrel . . . for rose-turning the mandrel is rotated slowly by means of a winch-driven pulley attached to the front of the lathe bed. A rosette fitted at the nose end of the mandrel has waves on the face in addition to those

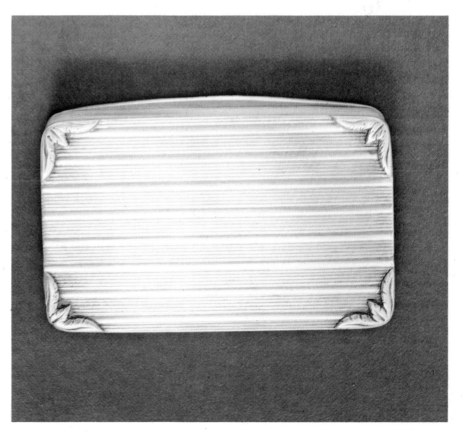

Above left
Victorian heavy silver-gilt snuffbox: the lid enriched with engraved floral motifs and with cast floral cartouche enclosing a pair of swans. With cast floral thumbpiece.
Maker: George Unite, Birmingham 1837.
Size: 2¾ inches by 1⅜ inches by ¾ of an inch deep.
George Unite was apprenticed to Joseph Willmore in 1810 for a period of eight years. He entered his 'GU' in a rectangular punch at Birmingham in 1830 and again in 1839. The shape of the punch was changed in 1861, when it appeared in a shield. The business was to continue well into the 1930's.

Lower left
William IV snuffbox: formed as finely cast and chased fox's mask.
Maker: Nathaniel Mills **ii**, Birmingham 1830.
Note: This is a rare subject; one of the few specimens noted was sold at Christie's in 1910, and was dated 1826, also by Mills.
Courtesy of the Birmingham Assay Office.

Right:
Top
Charles II large circular patchbox: engraved on the pull-off lid with 'tulip' motif.
Maker: **BC** (not known to Jackson) *circa* 1660.
Size: 2 inches in diameter by ¾ of an inch deep.

Upper left and right
William and Mary small circular patchbox: magnificently engraved on the pull-off lid and the base with 'Emblemata Amatoria' motifs. On the lid with a cherub firing an arrow at a pair of 'flaming hearts' on an altar, and on the base with a cherub placing a 'flaming heart' in a basket containing other hearts, and with amatory mottoes in French. With 'debased laurel wreath' borders.
Unmarked *circa* 1690.
Size: 1 inch in diameter by ¼ of an inch deep. This article and others in the same group has been discussed in the first chapter under the heading 'Amatory Subject Spiceboxes' and under 'Patchboxes' in the same chapter.

Lower left
Charles II oval spicebox: of large size. Engraved on the domical lid with cherub holding a rose, and the motto (in English) 'No rose without thorns'. With 'stand-away' hinge. Pricked inside the lid with fine contemporary cyphered monogram.
Maker: **DS** Crowned, *circa* 1680. (*vide* Jackson, page 481, line 12)
Size: 1½ inches by 1¼ inches by ⅝ of an inch deep.

Lower right
William and Mary oval spicebox: of small size. Engraved with foliate cartouche on the domed lid, and with 'stand-away' hinge, and with foliate motif on base.
Maker: John Albright, London *circa* 1690.
Size: 1 inch by ¾ of an inch by ⅝ of an inch deep.

Centre
William III rectangular cut-corner snuffbox: of small size, the lid finely engraved with scrolling acanthus foliage and with 'debased laurel' motif borders. With 'stand-away' 9-lugged hinge and projecting thumbpiece.
Maker's mark not clear: **I**— *circa* 1700. This
        M—
        ME
mark has been carefully checked and cannot be found at Goldsmiths' Hall.
Size: 2½ inches by 2 inches by ½ an inch deep.

on the edge . . . (speaking of another later German lathe) . . . The mandrel head-stock is hinged below and provided with a strong spring to keep any one of the several cams or rosettes in contact with a fixed rubber. The motion thus imparted to the mandrel caused a stationary cutting tool to produce on the work a wavy line or rosette instead of a true circle. By this means patterns suitable for decorating watch cases and snuff boxes could be produced'.

There were (and still are, as the methods are still in use which produced

Charles II sideways oval tobacco box: the lid engraved with manteled shield containing a stag's head. With light cable gadroon borders on lid and base.
Maker: **LS** Crowned, London 1675.
Size: 3¾ inches by 3 inches by ⅞ of an inch deep.
Courtesy of the Worshipful Company of Goldsmiths.

Charles II large oval tobacco box: with cable gadroon rims top and bottom. Engraved on the lid with elaborately manteled Coat-of-Arms incorporating a grated helmet in profile surmounting and surmounted by eaglets.
Maker: **RS** in Heart, London 1682.
Size: 4 inches by 3¼ inches by 1¼ inches deep.

William and Mary rectangular spice-casket: the slightly domed lid superlatively engraved with Chinoiserie motifs comprising: a 'debased laurel wreath' around the rim, palm leaves vertically engraved around the sides. and foliate scrolling motifs and a Chinese wearing a head-dress, on the lid. With small hinged 'bracket' handle and on 4 ball feet. The hinge (not shown) is of the 'stand-away' type.
Maker: Thomas Townley or Thomas Tucker (**TT** Crowned), London, *circa* 1690.
Size: $1\frac{7}{8}$ inches by $1\frac{1}{4}$ inches by $\frac{5}{8}$ of an inch deep.

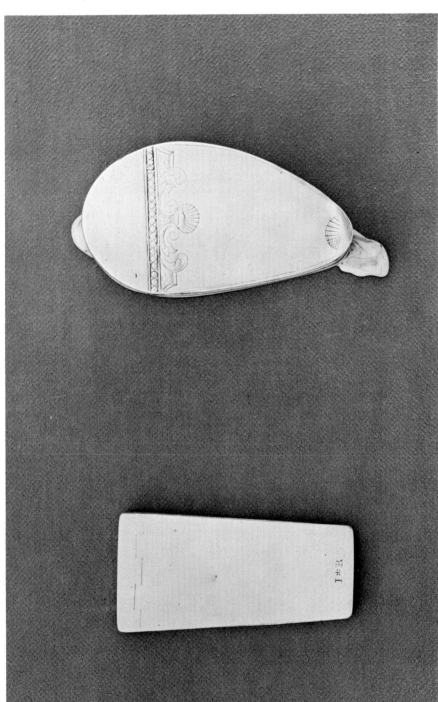

George II silver-mounted cowrie-shell snuff-box: formed from the 'teeth' of the mollusc. Engraved with 'architectural scroll and shell' motifs and with well-disguised 'integral' hinge, and reeded mounts.
Unmarked, *circa* 1730.
Size: $2\frac{1}{4}$ inches by $1\frac{1}{4}$ inches.

George III 'keystone' snuffbox: with finely constructed 'hidden-integral' hinge and of shallow form.
Unmarked, circa 1770, engraved with contemporary owner's initials.
This box is probably of Masonic origin, the 'keystone' being one of the symbols of the 'Mark Masons'.
Size: $2\frac{1}{8}$ inches by 1 inch by $\frac{1}{4}$ of an inch deep.

engine-turned patterns centuries ago) three main types of motifs as used in engine-turning:

(a) The 'Barleycorn' motif, which simulates an ear of barley, and produces the pattern over and over again.

(b) The 'Basketweave' motif, still the most popular of all, which is self-explanatory.

(c) The 'Fox's Head' motif, which depicted a group of three 'heads' or motifs arranged in the form of a 'arrow-head'. This motif was repeated over and over, to produce a satisfying pattern.

These three motifs were used to produce a wide variety of effects, either by eccentric or concentric cutting, resulting in geometrically accurate or distorted patterns, or by simple 'turning' resulting in alternating bands of 'wavy lines' and 'barleycorn' motifs, or 'wavy lines' alone, or various permutations. The most interesting use of engine-turning can best be seen on the Birmingham vinaigrettes which have architectural scene engravings on the lids. The very effective *chiaroscuro* device is simply radial engine-turning, and the engraving was applied on top of this. The early machines could do rotary, straight and oval work.

Four engine-turners working in Clerkenwell have been traced, and all were operative in the second decade of the 19th century, but the craft, of course, was at its height during the mid-Victorian period, in the 1840's and 50's. Not only the lids, but the sides and bases were engine-turned; the 'Fox's Head' motif is more common in French work than English and is dated *circa* 1830-70. Birmingham 'engine-cutters' as they were known in that illustrious city were also few in number, but presumably they had large establishments which were able to keep pace with the mass of work.

Queen Anne oval tobacco box: the lid embossed with heavy slant gadroon circlet embracing scalloped matted ground enriched with foliate motifs. With light twisted wire rims and reeded collet on base, and engraved with contemporary cyphers on lid.
Maker: Benjamin Bentley, London 1705.
Size: 3¾ inches by 3⅛ inches by 1 inch deep.
Currently in use by the Goldsmiths' Company as a toothpick box.
Courtesy of the Worshipful Company of Goldsmiths.

Opposite page:
Upper left
Victorian shaped rectangular vinaigrette: the lid hand-engraved with view of 'Brighthelmstone' (Brighton) showing the Old Chain Pier. On an engine-turned radial ground, with projecting foliate thumbpiece.
Maker: Nathaniel Mills **ii**, Birmingham 1847.
Size: 1½ inches by 1 inch.
The little 'pedestal-shaped' building in the foreground was the box-office where tickets were obtained for access to the pier. One then entered the gate on the left and proceeded to the pier, which was quite a way from the entrance, along the Marine Parade.

Above right
Victorian rectangular vinaigrette: hand-engraved with 'Blackfriars Bridge viewed from London Bridge' motif on lid, on an engine-turned radial background.
Maker: Nathaniel Mills **ii**, Birmingham 1846.
Size: 1⅜ inches by 1 inch.
This is a larger version of the 'incused sides' specimen also by Mills, but dated 1847.

Centre left
George III vertical oval vinaigrette: with 'stand-away' three-lugged hinge, the lid with bright-cut 'wriggle' motif and engraved contemporary crest in centre. Florally pierced grille.
Maker: Richard Lockwood, London 1800.
Size: 1 inch by ¾ of an inch.

Centre right
George III shallow rectangular vinaigrette: the lid engraved with central elliptical escutcheon containing 'abstract' motif, the side panels containing bright-cut foliate motifs.
Maker: Joseph Willmore, Birmingham 1810.
Size: 1¾ inches by ¾ of an inch.
Note: the 'abstract' motif has been noted on French 'gold piqué-inlay' boxes of *circa* 1780.

Lower left
George III large rectangular vinaigrette: the lid superbly hand-engraved with 'Shearing Scene' on a 'double-dot' ground. With projecting thumbpiece. Fine shell and filigree stamped grille.
Makers: Thropp and Taylor, Birmingham 1812.
Size: 1½ inches by 1¼ inches.

Lower right
George III small rectangular vinaigrette: the lid hand-engraved with 'Man in gig' motif on a 'double-dot' scored ground, with 'stand-away' hinge and projecting thumbpieces.
Maker: Samuel Pemberton **vi**, Birmingham 1811.
Size: 1 inch by ¾ of an inch.

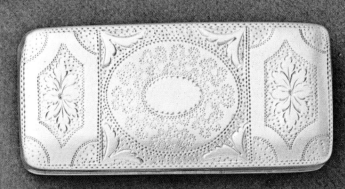

The suspicion which immediately comes to mind on beholding a boxlid enriched with an inserted plaquette, as on most 'repoussé-subject' boxes, is that this might have been mass-produced by the use of a die-struck motif, and, indeed, there appears to be no reason to doubt this belief. The fact that only a few specimens of a certain subject survive, while many hundreds of another subject remain extant, merely indicates the popularity of the latter, and the intervention of such factors as emigration, accident, and hoarding, which restrict the availability of the former. Furthermore, as was the case with most small articles, little value was placed upon these, and it is only nowadays, when values have appreciated beyond imagination, that many hitherto unknown subjects have been brought to light.

The early distinction has to be drawn between *repoussé and embossed work*, which could be done by hand (as described below in citing Theophilus' method, but which, in relation to most 19th century boxes, were struck in a die), and *hand-chasing*, which appears to be a type of repoussé, but which is, in reality, a hand-raised enrichment, effected by careful hammerwork struck on the top surface of the metal, to depress the surrounding silver, and thus heighten the motif. All three forms are listed here, as they are very often mistaken for each other. In repoussé-work and embossing, the plaquette was 'punched out' so that the 'high places' appeared to stand away from the background, again providing some feeling of depth. The two terms are here applied to 'deep perspective', (the former) and 'shallow perspective' (the latter), although both were applied by mechanical means.

The text is here interrupted briefly for the inclusion of an analysis of the enrichment on the finely hand-chased silver-gilt snuffbox bearing Freemasonic emblems. It is placed under the general subject heading for two reasons: firstly, that the method of hand-chasing for the *chiaroscuro* effect is about to be examined, and

6. Repoussé & Embossing

Freemasonic Boxes

Glasgow & Ajax.

Victorian large vertical cheroot case: the sides, lid and base finely hand-engraved with contemporary coaching and sailing themes and other like motifs. Engraved overall with scrolling acanthus foliage.
Maker: John Timms, Birmingham 1844.
Size: 5½ inches by 4¼ inches by 1½ inches deep.
Stella Margetson, in her interesting account of the old days of coaching *Journey by Stages* (published by Cassell in 1967) recalls something of the splendour of the 'Red Rover' Coach depicted on the side of this finely engraved box. 'The 'Red Rover' to Manchester, besides being painted scarlet, was decked out with red harness for the horses and red coats for the guard and coachman, and when Sherman of the Bull and Mouth (Edward Sherman, who ran a rival service) succeeded in running the 'Red Rover' off the road, Robert Nelson promptly started a new fast coach called the 'Beehive', with superior accommodation for comfort and safety to any coach in Europe.

Edward Sherman had married three elderly widows in quick succession and, with the money they bequeathed to him, he acquired the old Bull and Mouth inn in St. Martin's-le-Grand, originally called the Boulogne Mouth in honour of Henry VIII's capture of Boulogne Harbour'.

It is not known what the 'Old Salopian' refers to, nor the 'Glasgow & Ajax', but this may have been a tea-clipper.

80

secondly, because the subject of 'Freemasonry' is of interest to a wide section of people. The insertion of snuff and other boxes bearing Masonic emblems, which are illustrated in this present work, has been made, not because the containers are directly connected with the Masonic rites, but because they are ordinary boxes with unusual 'Applied Ornament'—yet another essay into the craft of boxlid enrichment—and, furthermore, are of fine workmanship. In order not to offend the susceptibilities of readers who might be Freemasons, and thus resent the revelation of some of their esoteric rites, the details and meanings of the symbols have been kept to a minimum, and the vagueness is therefore deliberate.

The silver-gilt snuffbox is doubly uncommon. Firstly, it is the result of a 'marriage' between an English box, by John Phipps, who entered his mark at Goldsmiths' Hall in 1767, and a French plaquette by the last surviving member of a famous French family of sculptors and copyists, Guillaume Coustos (1716-1777), and, secondly, the lid, being by a foreign artist, is signed. The item itself is a masterpiece of perspective 'on the flat', in which the central motif—a Masonic Temple—is supported on a 'stepped approach' with columns at either side and on a moulded plinth. The interior of the Temple is given depth by the use of a half-crescent device, which suggests a cupola, to which even further 'depth' is imparted by the suspended 'five-pointed Star of David incorporating the letter G' (which symbolises one of the seven 'Liberal Arts', the remaining six being: grammar, dialect, rhetoric, music, astronomy and arithmetic) and which has other Masonic connotations.

The design is given further form by the introduction of a baroque scrolling cartouche, which wanders in and out of the motifs and finally forms part of the 'stepped approach'. In addition to the other Masonic symbols—the *plumb-rule* on the left, which forms part of the Jewel of the Junior Grand Warden, and the *level* on the right, which is part of the Jewel of the Senior Grand Warden, the whole is

surmounted by the 'All-seeing Eye', which, to quote Bernard E. Jones's *Free-mason's Guide and Compendium*, is 'a symbol of very great antiquity representing the ever-watchful and omnipresent Deity and, as a Christian symbol, supported by a host of Biblical references. Even in its Masonic form of an open eye within a triangle, it has been used as a Church emblem, but it came to freemasonry much more probably from alchemy than from Christian symbolism'.

The resourceful craftsman who hand-chased this boxlid, finished his work by giving the background a liberal 'matt-chased' effect, by the use of a special punch, which strikes tiny 'dots' all over the surface. The letters 'M.M', in the bottom right-hand corner are not part of the signature, but refer to the original owner, who was a Master Mason.

To return to the original discussion on the subject of repoussé and embossed work, as has been stated, most 19th century boxlids were struck in machine dies. This mechanisation would explain the 'sameness' or uniformity of so many boxlid subjects, where the self-same scene appears on every box; thus, a shallow relief of one of the commonest subjects—Abbotsford House, the home of Sir Walter Scott—(mostly struck to mark the occasion of his death in 1832) will have the same Gothic turrets, chimneys, flag-tower and gardens as almost every other box enriched with this theme. A few specimens might bear some additional details such as the Gothic-arched wall, looking South-West, or trees to the left, but overall, the subject was faithfully copied by various makers.

The distinguished Birmingham elder-craftsman (whose views on the mech-anisation of ornament appear below, and form an important contribution to current knowledge), on being asked about the possible identity of the Birmingham die-makers, replied that his father had told him, that in *his* youth (the firm goes back to the 1880's) 'there were individuals who were extremely clever in copying the work of others, in the early days'. This statement, of course, implies that there *were* original inventors and adaptors (full details of these and their patents appear below) but, in essence, it is the age-old story of the piracy of one man's work by twenty others . . .

Of course, die-making for repoussé-work is by no means a modern invention: quite apart from the Simon van de Passe counters which were struck in an intaglio die (as stated above), the great 12th century Benedictine monk, Theophilus, in his famous Treatise (also mentioned above) set forth his detailed instructions for this device. Translations from the original Latin text are twelve in number. The first English translation was by Robert Hendrie, published in 1847 by John Murray, but this, and subsequent versions, have been superseded by an admirably

Theophilus' Method of Die-Stamping

George III small plain octagonal snuff box: with 'sunken-integral' hinge and plain up-bending thumbpiece. Engraved with 'Garter' motif on lid.
Makers: Simpson & Son, Birmingham, 1812.

George IV small engraved-top snuff box: hand-engraved with 'University College, Oxford' on the lid, and 'chevron' motifs to mask the 'sunken-integral' hinge.
Makers: William Postans & George Tye, Birmingham, 1823. This box is mentioned in the text.
Courtesy of the Birmingham Assay Office.

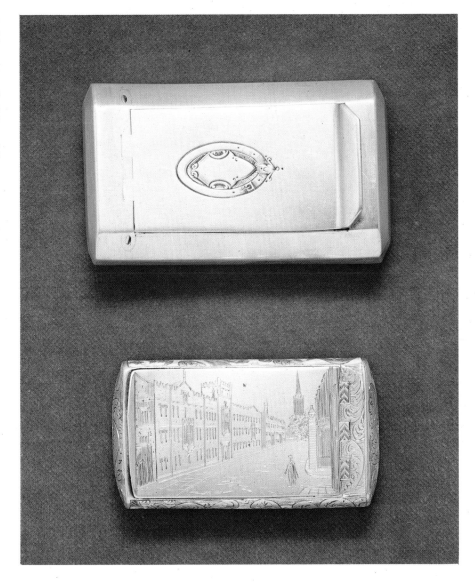

George III shallow rectangular snuff box: with twin lids, opening away from each other. Engraved on one lid with a 'laurel wreath' and on the other with a contemporary monogram.
Maker: Hester Bateman, London 1788.
Size: 3 inches by 2¼ inches by ½ an inch deep.

George I flat vertical snuff box: the lid engraved with 'architectural' motifs—scrolls and scales—interspersed with floral terminals. The 'hidden-integral' hinge masked by band of 'band-motives' in a straight line, which is repeated at the other end, near the projecting thumbpiece.
Maker: Starling Wilford, London *circa* 1720. (Maker's mark and lion passant only).
Size: 3¾ inches by 2⅛ inches by ¼ of an inch deep.

researched work *On Divers Arts* by John G. Hawthorne and Cyril Stanley Smith, published by the University of Chicago Press in 1963. This finely balanced analysis, in addition to the actual translation, traces Theophilus' origins, by comparative methods, using the work of the earlier translators, to the 12th century German monk, Roger of Helmarshausen. The work, they believe, was written between 1110-40, and Roger used the pseudonym 'Theophilus' because it had a Byzantine sound, to identify himself with the Byzantine methods he admired and described.

In their footnote to Theophilus' method of *De Opere Quod Sigillis Imprimitur* or, *Of Work which is Impressed with Stamps* (here dealing with embossing or repoussé-work by primitive mechanical means) they say the following: 'This process of putting repetitive designs on thin sheet metal by pressing it against a carved form of a harder metal or stone is of great antiquity and ubiquity. It has been employed particularly to make small decorations out of extremely thin gold, and such objects may be seen among artefacts from ancient Mesopotamia, Egypt, Mycenae, and Etruria, as well as from the pre-Columbian New World. The product, though sparing of the precious metal and labour, looks flashy but cheap and is easily subject to damage'.

In passing, it is ironic that Hendrie in the footnote of his translation on the same topic, also comments on this, and continues that he had seen designs executed in Paris, in thin gilt copper, where the method of die-stamping was 'a simple lever, fitted upon a tall upright post, with a weight attached at one end; the other extremity of the lever was pulled by a rope. Our Birmingham and Sheffield manufacturers, could, were proper designs procured from our artists, defy all attempts at competition, and re-establish a neglected source of profit and industry'. Hendrie was thus obviously unaware that this very method, much mechanised, was in contemporary use by many Birmingham *and* Sheffield craftsmen, and had been for at least a decade!

Victorian vertical shaped rectangular card-case; the centre with repoussé view of the Crystal Palace in high relief, and with repoussé foliate motifs around rim.
Maker: W. Dudley, Birmingham 1850.
Size: 4 inches by 3 inches.
W. Dudley entered his mark at Birmingham in 1848 and was working until 1868.

Victorian tobacco-cum-pipecase: of rectangular shape and finely hand-engraved overall with scrolling foliate motifs, and with heavily cast foliate border. The rectangular lid protects the tobacco compartment, the side lid—the pipecase, and the base has a compartment for vestas, that is, wax matches, which are first mentioned in use *circa* 1839; and owed their name to Vesta, the Roman goddess of hearth and household. This receptacle would accommodate a medium-sized clay-pipe. Well disguised 'integral hinge'.
Maker: W. R. Smiley, London, 1855.
Size: 5 inches by 2½ inches by 1¼ inches deep.

Victorian vertical rectangular cardcase: hand-engraved with view of Sir Walter Scott's home 'Abbotsford House', on a concentric engine-turned ground. Set in a scrolling floral cartouche and with castellated towers in all four corners, enriched with further concentric engine-turning.
Maker: Nathaniel Mills **ii**, Birmingham 1840.
Size: 4 inches by 3 inches.

Victorian silver-gilt superbly hand-engraved vinaigrette: formed as a book, the lid and base forming the 'covers'. The lid engraved with a vertical panel depicting a floral arrangement in a vase, around which two birds fly, the whole supported on a console. The perimeter of the panel engraved with scrolling acanthus foliage. The 'back-cover' similarly embellished with a panel containing a 'tulip and butterfly' motif. Engraved along the back to simulate a 'book-spine' with 'souvenir' on a label. With a finely hand-pierced grille.
Makers: Rawlings and Summer, London, 1840.
Size: 1½ inches by 1 inch by ¼ of an inch deep.

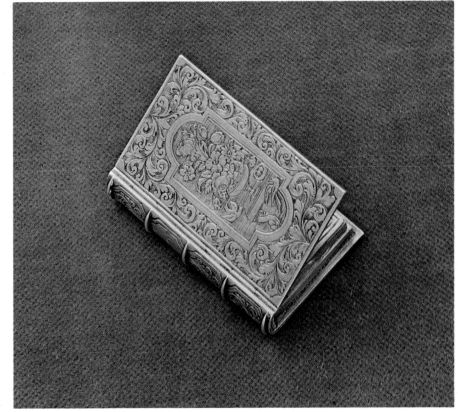

Victorian small rectangular vinaigrette: with incused sides, the lid hand-engraved with 'Blackfriars Bridge, viewed from London Bridge' with St. Paul's in the background, on an engine-turned radial ground.
Maker: Nathaniel Mills **ii**, Birmingham 1847.
Size: 1 inch by ¾ of an inch.

George III vertically engraved vinaigrette: subject: 'The Lavender Seller', hand-engraved in imitation of a 'Cries of London' subject.
Maker: Matthew Linwood **v**, Birmingham 1813.
Size: 1 inch by ¾ of an inch.

George III large rectangular vinaigrette: of very shallow form, hand-engraved on the lid with 'Hare in Den' subject (after Thomas Bewick).
Maker: Samuel Pemberton **vi**, Birmingham 1809.
Size: 1¾ inches by 1¼ inches.
This specimen is mentioned in the text.

In order to return to Theophilus' own description of repoussé-work, it is first necessary to point out that the technique as seen by him, referred to hand-ornament raised by hammering from the back of the sheet of metal, and must be distinguished from his technique of 'striking in a die' as described by Hawthorne and Smith. It is included in this survey because of its unique mediaeval origin. In order to preserve the feeling of 'antiquity', Hendrie's version is used, although Hawthorne and Smith's translation is much smoother, and probably the more correct. The parentheses are the present writer's.

Theophilus begins: '*Percute tabulam auream sive argenteam quantae longitudinis et latitudinis velis ad elevendas imagines*'—Beat a gold or silver plate as long and wide as you wish for relieving the figures . . . (directions are given for testing the quality of the casting) . . . when it has become so (sound, and reliable to work on) see beforehand that the anvils and your hammers, with which you should work, are quite smooth and polished; and take care that the gold or silver plate be so equally thinned everywhere, that it be in no place thicker than in another. And when it has been thinned so that the nail, slightly pressed upon it, may show upon the other side, and it is perfectly sound, directly portray the figures you may wish, according to your will . . . you will then with a curved iron, well polished, gently however, rub the head in the first place, which must be more raised; and so turning the plate upon the right side you will rub around the head, also with the smooth and polished iron so that the ground may descend and the head be raised, and you will directly beat around the head with a middling sized hammer upon the anvil, gently, and you thus cook it before the furnace, until it glows, coals being superposed in that place. Which being done, and the plate cooled by itself, you will again rub it with the curved instrument on the underneath part, inside the hollow of the head, slightly and carefully, and turning the plate you will again rub with the smooth iron upon the upper part, and you depress the ground that the relief of the head may be raised, and

William IV rectangular vinaigrette: the lid finely hand-engraved with 'Griffin amidst foliate scrolls' motif, and with fine 'integral-hinge' and cast foliate thumbpiece.
Makers: Rawlings and Sumner, London 1830.
Size: 1⅝ inches by 1¼ inches.

William and Mary silver-mounted oval tobacco box: the lid and base composed of finely carved boxwood plaques. The lid, set in a scalloped rim which is pinned into position, is carved with the arms of the Worshipful Company of Plumbers, and the owner's initials 'FH'.

Unmarked *circa* 1690.

Size: 4¾ inches by 3½ inches by 1 inch deep.

Before becoming a Member of the Guild, this owner would have to be apprenticed. The original documents relating to the Plumbers' Company are in the custody of the Guildhall Library, London, and during the period recording apprenticeships between 1660 to 1720, two apprentices with the initials 'FH' appear, namely:

Francis Heild, apprenticed 2nd March 1662
Francis Hoad, apprenticed 29th June 1667

Previous page: Upper left
George III shaped vinaigrette: of 'cushion-shape', with slightly projecting thumbpiece.
Maker: Matthew Linwood **v**, Birmingham 1811.
Size: 1 inch by ¾ of an inch.

Upper right
George III shaped vinaigrette: formed as 'raying shell', with slightly projecting thumb-piece.
Maker: Matthew Linwood **v**, Birmingham 1806.
Size: 1 inch by ¾ of an inch.

Centre left
George III shaped vinaigrette: formed as Crown. Bright-cut with 'double-dot scoring' and foliate and diaper motifs. 'Stand-away' hinge.
Makers: Simpson and Son, Birmingham 1819.
Size: ¾ of an inch by ⅝ of an inch.
This is a variation of the more common Willmore 'Crown' made to commemorate the Coronation of George IV in 1820.

Centre right
George III shaped vinaigrette: formed as a 'Horseshoe'. The lid engraved with three bands of foliate motifs. With slightly projecting thumbpiece.
Makers: Cocks and Bettridge, Birmingham 1811.
Size: 1 inch by ¾ of an inch.

Lower left
Victorian shaped vinaigrette: formed as 'Musselshell', of cast form and with 'integral-hinge' and suspensory loop.
Maker: Samson Mordan, London 1876.
Size: 1¾ inches by ¾ of an inch.

Lower right
George IV circular vinaigrette: formed as a 'watch'. The lid with cast 'forget-me-not' motif set with turquoises, and cast foliate border. With similarly enriched suspensory loop handle.
Maker: Thomas Newbold, Birmingham 1820.
Size: 1 inch in diameter by ¼ of an inch deep.

again gently striking it with the middling hammer about this, you recook it, by applying the coals; and thus you act often, by carefully raising it inside and outside and frequently hammering, as often cooking until the relief is brought to the height of three or four fingers, or more or less, according to the number of figures'. The remainder of Theophilus' instructions concern the design and execution of the details—the mouth, nose and eyes—and methods of re-soldering fractures should these occur, and how to polish the plate and apply gilding to it.

Birmingham Repoussé-Work

How were the Birmingham dies for mechanical striking made and by whom? The first part of the question is easily answered: the subject, whatever it was to be, was first copied by an artist from a contemporary painting, engraving or print, probably the last. It was then passed to a craftsman-engraver, who scooped out the pattern in a block of hard steel (almost as the Birmingham craftsmen who were interviewed still do today) and a refinement of Theophilus' method was then applied, the one important difference being the use of power-operated machines—water-power, of course—and the boxlid was then 'chased up' by hand, to remove any excess metal and to heighten the effect of 'depth'. After being polished, it was trimmed and inserted into the boxlid.

George III silver-mounted elliptical snuffbox: the lid with well constructed 'integral-hinge' and of slightly domical form, the container of 'Pontypool Japanware', originally of a dark green colour, with a band of gold around the rim. The lid inscribed: 'John Evans Born 25 March 1772', and fully hall-marked inside.
Makers: Phipps and Robinson, London 1805.
Size: 3 inches by 1⅝ inches by ¾ of an inch deep.

'Pontypool Japanware' was invented *circa* 1728 by Thomas Allgood, the manager of the Pontypool Ironworks, owned by the Hanbury family. Allgood also invented a method of tinning iron sheets, and this led to the perfection of the method of lacquering on the tinned plates. Soon, the Pontypool Japan factory was opened as a separate works by Edward Allgood. The first building chosen was at the bottom of Trosnant, a suburb of Pontypool, and here Edward Allgood and his sons, with their wives and children, worked together keeping the process a family secret. This snuffbox was made during the life of Billy Allgood, one of the sons, who died in 1813, and the business finally closed in 1822. Many fine articles were made in this pleasant medium, and included beautifully painted trays, baskets, teapots and coffee-pots. Billy Allgood claimed that many of his best pieces were 'stoved' that is, baked in an oven, from as much as twelve to sixteen times, rubbed down with pumice powder, and relacquered until the iron plate and the lacquer had become as one, almost like Battersea Enamel but without its fragility. Various colours, too, were introduced, a rare shade of blue, for instance, as well as various shades of red, from sealing-wax red to deep crimson or ruby.

George III silver-mounted leather snuffbox: of vertical cut-corner rectangular variety. The lid mounted with silver cut-corner escutcheon engraved with owner's monogram and 'Rockhampton'. Three-lugged silver applied hinge.
Unmarked *circa* 1770.
Size: 4 inches by 2½ inches by ¾ of an inch deep.

Leather was used for decorative and practical purposes from very early days. As John Waterer explains in his *Leather* issued by the Museum of Leathercraft in 1956, 'It is interesting that leather has always been used primarily because it was the best—and in some instances the only suitable—material for a given purpose . . . at an early date, for example, it was employed in sling seats, as in the 'X' chair, and for backs, Spanish leather being sometimes so employed. Leather 'carpets', that is to say, covers for furniture such as beds and tables, are mentioned as early as 1423 in an inventory of the wardrobe of Henry VI, being made of Spanish leather . . . large numbers . . . of containers still exist. The finest were individual cases into which the objects for which they were specifically made fitted snugly . . . they were made to hold precious books, reliquaries, jewels, knives and scissors, daggers, clocks, astronomical instruments and Church Plate'.

Few tangible clues remain on the identity of the die-sinkers. William West's *The History, Topography and Directory of Warwickshire*, which has a large section on Birmingham and its craftsmen, lists no fewer than forty-eight die-sinkers, of whom only one, in 1830, is also identifiable as a silversmith. This was Edward Thomason, but he was no mere 'small-worker': he had, next to Matthew Boulton, the largest manufactory in Birmingham, and produced a bewildering variety of articles, among which were medals, so perhaps the dies were used for these. It is probable that, as in the case of the engravers mentioned above, die-sinkers who worked on seals also produced dies for the silversmiths; when a new subject was introduced, all the other die-makers copied it and distributed the motif to all who requested it.

Of the *genre* of the subjects, also, little can be traced. But there are a few slender clues, which coincidence has brought to light. Most boxes which have 'Sporting Subjects' enrichment are of the cast variety, probably because casting was more to the taste of the wealthy, as a symbol of opulence, but towards the middle of the 19th century, repoussé-top boxes with this type of subject may be found. One such box had a 'Hunting-scene' subject, which, by pure chance, was also noted on an engraved box by Joseph Willmore, dated *circa* 1820, which was exhibited at the British Antique Dealers' Fair in 1954. This latter box was discussed in an article in *Apollo Magazine*, by G. Bernard Hughes, who attributed the subject to Henry Alken, the great English etcher (1784–1851) who specialised in both sporting subjects and caricatures of them. The subject was 'In Full Cry', and the central figure was a mounted huntsman beckoning his fellows on. The same motif was subsequently noted on a Victorian box, dated 1840, but this was a repoussé-top specimen. So a probable source for these 'Sporting Subjects' may be found among works on this type of painting. It is possible that further hitherto unknown subjects may be identified with the use of such books as Lord Lavington's *Sporting Pictures at Lavington Park*, (printed for private circulation in 1927), which illustrates many pictures by various famous artists in this *genre*, and other similar works.

Another interesting ascription was discovered, again by pure accident, when a water-colour by Joseph Nash dated 1846, the subject of which was Buckingham Palace with the Marble Arch still in front (it was removed to its present site at Tyburn in 1851) was noted. On closer examination, the subject turned out to be the exact facsimile of the superb table snuffbox, illustrated on page 98 of *Investing in Silver*, which is by Nathaniel Mills. Subsequently, two other articles—a sweetmeat basket and the covers of an 'aide memoire'—were also observed to bear the same subject, all three dated 1846 and by the same maker.

William III oval silver-mounted tortoiseshell tobacco box: the panels set in scalloped rims, top and bottom, and with encircling rib around body. The lift-off lid engraved with 'debased laurel wreath' border and the owner's initials in cyphered form and intertwining scrolls. The base engraved with the owner's name 'John Collier' and the name of his home-town 'Bristol', both in scrolling characters, the latter in cyphered characters.
Unmarked, *circa* 1700.
Size: 4½ inches by 3¼ inches by 1 inch deep.
John Collier, son of John Collier, of Blagdon, Somerset, yeoman, was apprenticed to Robert Godfrey, barber-surgeon, on the 8th of April 1689. He was made a Burgess of Bristol in December 1698 and was living in the parish of St. Michael in that city as late as 1722.
Illustrated are views of the top and base of the box, as well as one exhibiting the fine translucent tortoiseshell panel which constitutes the base.

Such fortuitious discoveries, however, are rare, and furthermore, artistic licence has also to be taken into account. Very often, a view of a castle, or a famous country house or mansion is shown out of context, with only one aspect receiving attention. The Terrace at Windsor Castle, for instance, was for years mistaken for a view of the buildings at Hampton Court, because there was not enough detail to identify the scene with the former, but the subject seemed to comply with the architecture of the latter. For the most part, views in the 'Castles, Cathedrals and Country-house series were probably struck (as was stated in *Investing in Silver*, pages 113–4) to serve as mementoes of visits to well-known places by a public which was just beginning to savour the delights of unlimited rail travel.

The realisation that there might be mechanical forces at work on what had hitherto been believed to be 'hand-engraved' ornament came gradually, following a series of fortunate coincidences. A number of the famous Matthew Linwood series 'Admiral Lord Nelson' vinaigrettes (which portray, on the lid, the Hero of Trafalgar in his characteristic pose with the sleeve pinned up and the motto 'England expects every man will do his duty') were observed over a period of about eight years. On noting that perhaps the second specimen had a peculiar 'vagueness' about one certain position near the top of the head, a watch was thereafter maintained, and subsequent examples revealed the same anomaly—a fact which could not be explained away by the convenient phrase 'wear and tear'—and it did not make sense for one particular spot to be so lightly engraved as to make the subject almost invisible. When this present work was being researched, therefore, a photograph of one of these 'Nelson Vinaigrettes' was submitted to the senior Birmingham engraver mentioned above, who immediately and unhesitatingly identified it as a specimen of 'Die-stamping'.

George III rectangular silver-mounted snuff-box: in hand-carved walnut, with twin sideways opening lids, inset with silver plates bearing armorial crests of the Puleston family of Flintshire. The top carved with bosses in Renaissance style, upon a matted ground, the body with British National Emblems: Rose, Shamrock and Thistle, and on each corner with head of King George III. The base with similar enrichment to the top.
Unmarked *circa* 1813.
Size: 5 inches by 2¾ inches by 2⅝ inches deep.

7. Die-Stamping

The Puleston line began *circa* 1220 and was originally written 'De Pyveleston'. It was then seated at Emral, County Flint. The baronetcy of which this box was probably a commemorative relic, was granted in 1813, and the Prince of Wales Feathers on the Arms were in commemoration of Sir Richard Puleston's having had the honour of introducing the Prince of Wales into the principality on the 9th of September, 1806. Sir Richard Price, born in 1765, who inherited the estates of his maternal family, assumed in 1812 the surname of Puleston, and was created a baronet in November 1813. The baronetcy became extinct in 1898.

Upper left
William IV oval vinaigrette: the lid has inserted carved cameo plaque. Subject: Venus and Cupid. With cast foliate border, the sides enriched with cast diaper motifs.
Maker: Nathaniel Mills **ii**, Birmingham 1836.
Size: 1⅝ inches by 1¼ inches.
Carved Cameo subjects are mentioned in the text.

Upper right
Victorian oval vinaigrette: with shaped lid set with agate plaque. The border and base enriched with engraved 'wriggle' and foliate motifs, and with suspensory loop.
Maker: F. Marston, Birmingham 1875.
Size: 1½ inches by 1 inch.
Marston entered his mark at Birmingham in 1843 and was working till 1896.

Lower left
George III silver-mounted cowrie-shell vinaigrette: of the genus *Cypraea Arabica*, with finely pierced 'quatrefoil and diaper' grille. The shaped oval elliptical lid plain.
Maker: Joseph Willmore, Birmingham 1809.
Size: 1 inch by ¾ of an inch.
As has been stated in the Willmore Genealogy, Joseph **ii** entered his mark at the Birmingham Assay Office *circa* 1808; this article, therefore, must be one of his earliest pieces, and, indeed, none earlier has been noted.

Lower right
William IV rectangular vinaigrette: silver-gilt, hand-engraved with scrolling foliate motifs, the lid set with 'blister-pearl' mounted as a papillon dog, the sides slightly incurving.
Maker: James Beebe, London 1836.
Size: 1½ inches by 1⅛ inches.
Barry Clifford, writing in *The Book of the Dog*, states: 'It would appear that . . . the breed . . . . was one of the first essentially European races to be taken to the Americas by the early Spanish settlers, and may well have been part ancestors of the Mexican chihuahuas'. A very rare specimen.

Victorian snuffbox: the lid carved in mother-of-pearl with view of Birmingham Town Hall. This fine building was designed by Joseph Hansom (who also invented the cab named after him) and is modelled on the Temple of Castor and Pollux in Rome. It was completed in 1850, so this box must have been made to celebrate its foundation.
Maker: Francis Clark, Birmingham, 1839.
The base and sides engine-turned.
Courtesy of the Birmingham Assay Office.

Were it not for the discovery of a contemporary patent for a method of *Cutting, Pressing and Squeezing Metals, etc* taken out in 1804 by John Gregory Hancock of Birmingham, a die-engraver by profession, which was first noted in Bennet Woodcroft's *Subject-matter Index of Patents of Inventions*, London 1857, the attention of the writer would not have been focussed on the method at all, but on reflection, Hancock's invention deals not so much with a completely new invention for stamping metal—after all, we have read Theophilus' method—as with a method of (to quote the official description on the patent-specification)

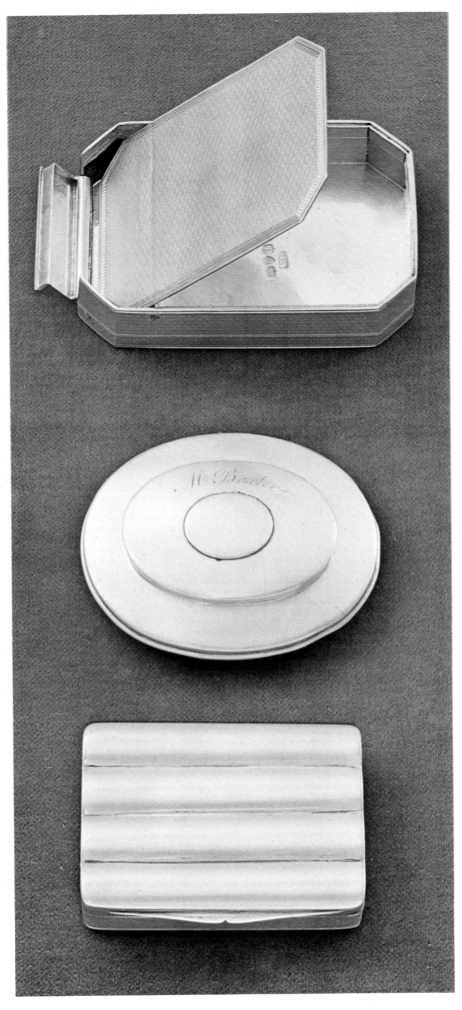

William IV rectangular cut-corner 'trick snuffbox': enriched overall with engine-turning, and with 'simulated hinges' to deceive the eye. The mechanism of the masked lid is on a hinged pivot which is placed about ¾ of an inch away from the drop-down hinged flange forming the false end of the rectangle. When the lid is closed and the flange replaced, little can be seen of the method of opening.
Maker: Edward Edwards, London, 1831.
Size: 3⅛ inches by 1⅞ inches by ¾ of an inch deep.

George III oval snuffbox: the lid formed as a raised ellipse on a shallow bezel, and with heavy encircling rib around body.
Maker: John Robertson, Newcastle, *circa* 1790. In keeping with other articles from this assay office (where marking anomalies are frequently found) this specimen is only partially marked, lacking both the town-mark and the date-letter. The outline of the lion passant (which is struck in a straight cartouche) and the 'shaped to the outline' of the King's Head, indicate its Newcastle origins.
Engraved with contemporary owner's name.
Size: 2⅝ inches by 2 inches.

George III heavy gauge snuffbox: the lid and base enriched with 'ridged' corrugations, and with simple thumbpiece.
Maker: William Pugh, Birmingham, 1810.
Size: 2⅜ inches by 1½ inches.

Forcing or working the bolts of presses or of engines used for the purpose of cutting, pressing, and squeezing,' etc. . Nevertheless, the method of die-stamping metal was refined, and it is odd that Linwood appears to be the first person to have used 'die-stamped ornament' on his boxes.

It ought, at this juncture, to be pointed out that when speaking of boxmakers, and the Birmingham craftsmen in particular, it should be borne in mind that with the exception of the very large manufactories (Thomason has been mentioned above) most workshops employed 'outworkers' for all but the essential silversmithing work. Thus, a box would be made by Linwood, who sent it out to receive the hinge, which was made by a specialist 'hinge-maker', then to be engraved or bright-cut by another specialist. The grilles were pierced (or as has recently been discovered through pure coincidence) die-stamped. A very fine caddy-spoon by John Barber of Birmingham, dated 1823 was found to have, as part of the enrichment in the 'shovel-bowl', a fully recognisable vinaigrette grille die-stamped in the centre. The grille had all the characteristics of the usual 'box-grille', namely, floral motifs and a central 'snowdrop' motif, but it was completely unpierced. A closer examination of some of Linwood's so-called 'filigree grilles' has also revealed that only the front looks like filigree, the back is quite flat, so that these, too, were struck in a die to simulate other methods of silversmithing. It should be emphasised that these latter specimens should not be confused with the 'simulated filigree' enrichment on caddy-spoons, where the ornament merely *looks like* filigree in its delicate piercing; in this case, the filigree-effect is so real that unless the back of the plate can be examined, the deception is complete.

When the various components were returned to the original maker, he assembled them and sent the article for assay: thus, only his mark appears. Hand-pierced grilles appear to have arrived *circa* 1840.

George III vertically 'die-stamped' vinaigrette subject: 'Admiral Lord Nelson' with the motto 'England expects Every Man Will Do His Duty' engraved in an oval. On a 'scored threaded' ground. With 'integral-hinge' and short scrolling thumbpiece. The grille die stamped with view of 'The Victory' and the date of the Battle of Trafalgar 'Oct. 21 1805'. Engraved on the base with a floral motif. Maker: Matthew Linwood **v,** Birmingham, 1806.
Size: 1¼ inches by 1 inch.
This article is mentioned in the text.

Victorian shaped rectangular vinaigrette: subject: York Minster. 'Die-stamped' on an horizontally engine-turned ground, with hints of hand engraved foliage at rims.
Maker: Nathaniel Mills **ii,** Birmingham 1850.
Size: 1½ inches by 1¼ inches.
This article is mentioned in the text.

Right
William IV silver-mounted cowrie-shell: of large size formed as a snuff box. The lid finely engine-turned in alternating bands of 'Barley-corn' and 'wave' motifs, and with plain escutcheon in centre containing a crest. The thumbpiece of the shaped scrolling variety.
Maker: G. Read, London, 1833.
Size: 3½ inches by 2¼ inches.
This maker is not recorded in Jackson, but is in the Register at Goldsmiths' Hall, where his address is given as '18 Cock Lane, Hatton Garden'. He entered his mark on the 11th of March 1830.

George III oval elliptical snuffbox: the lid
with inserted mother-of-pearl plaque enriched
in centre with silver oval plate which is
engraved with Masonic subjects: squares and
compasses, an arch composed of two Doric
columns and further Masonic symbols in a
squared pavement. The lid enriched with
band of reeding and with scrolling thumbpiece.
Maker: Thomas Bowen, London 1800.
Size: 3½ inches by 2½ inches by 1 inch deep.
Thomas Bowen entered his mark at Goldsmiths' Hall in 1782. He worked at 5 Naked
Boy Court, Ludgate Hill.
Courtesy of the Board of General Purposes, Free-
masons' Hall.

George III silver-mounted cowrie-shell snuffbox: the lid with 'integral-hinge' and engraved
with Masonic subjects—square and compasses,
sun, moon and stars, the All-Seeing Eye, and
other Masonic emblems of symbolic signifi-
cance.
Maker: Joseph Taylor, Birmingham 1810.
Size: 2¾ inches by 2 inches.
Cowrie-shell boxes from the workshop of
Joseph Taylor are uncommon.
Courtesy of the Board of General Purposes, Free-
masons' Hall.

George III oval vertical tobacco box: the
inserted domed plaque of the lid enriched with
Freemasonic subjects—the All-Seeing Eye
within an arch, resting on Corinthian and
Doric columns, on which stand figures representing Faith, Hope and Charity, clasped
hands symbolic of friendship, a 'Star of David'
containing the 'G' for geometry, and other
Masonic symbols on a squared pavement. The
skull in the far background symbolising
mortality.
Maker: John Robertson, Newcastle *circa* 1790.
Size: 4 inches by 3 inches by 1¼ inches deep.
John Robertson's association with Thomas
Bewick has been mentioned in the text, but it
is not certain that this box was engraved by
him; if it did pass through his workshop, it
might have been executed by one of Bewick's
pupils.
Courtesy of the Board of General Purposes, Free-
masons' Hall.

Left
George III large circular toilet-box: with
pull-off lid, the perimeter bright-cut with
foliate motifs, the interior of the lid with
swags and festoons of foliage and Coat-of-
Arms in a shield, the base engraved with
Masonic theme—level, square and compasses
and rule—and the date '1784'.
Makers: Phipps and Robinson, London, 1784.
Size: 5¼ inches in diameter by 1 inch deep.
This box has no Masonic purpose and is regarded as a 'Presentation Piece' probably given
to the recipient, William Cresswell in token of
some service to his lodge.
Courtesy the Board of General Purposes, Free-
masons' Hall.

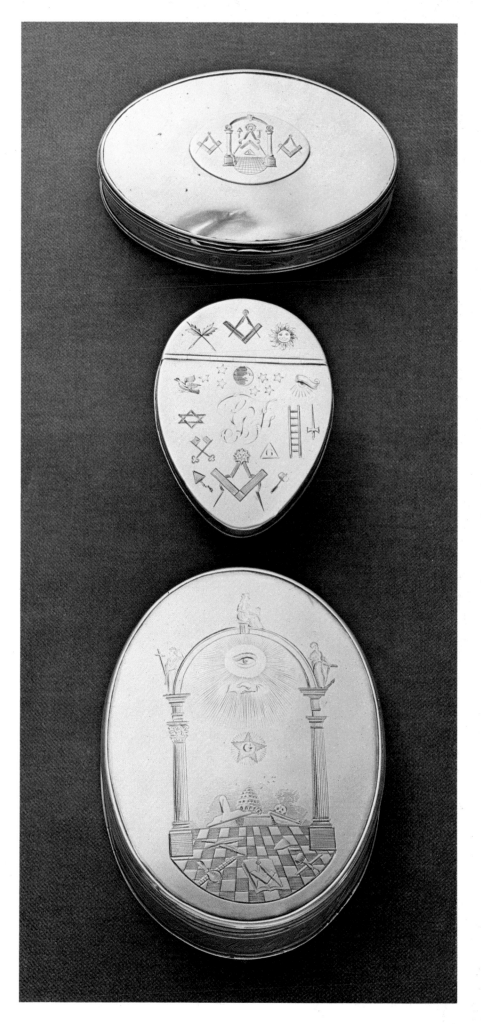

George III circular snuffbox: silver-gilt with pull-off lid. The lid enriched with repoussé Arms of the Chevalier Bartholomew Ruspini. Maker: Charles March, London 1786.
Size: 2¼ inches in diameter by ⅝ of an inch deep.

The Chevalier Ruspini was both a distinguished Freemason and a noted dentist. He founded the Royal Masonic Institution for Girls in 1788, and this box has passed into the possession of the Grand Lodge Museum. He invented and sold tins of dentifrice closely resembling this box. The Coat-of-Arms and address exactly imitates one of these base metal receptacles, and it is therefore probable that this silver specimen was made for Ruspini himself to be used as a snuffbox, and not as a dentifrice box, as has been believed hitherto. A full account of the Chevalier Ruspini and his philanthropic work can be found in J. Menzies Campbell's *Dentistry Then and Now* (published privately by the author, 1963).
Courtesy of the Board of General Purposes, Freemasons' Hall.

George III rectangular snuffbox: silver-gilt, the lid with inserted hand-chased plaque enriched with Masonic subjects. With 'integral hinge' and simple scrolling thumbpiece.
Makers: John Phipps, London *circa* 1770 (box)
Guillaume Coustos, Paris *circa* 1770 (plaque)
Size: 3⅜ inches by 2⅝ inches by ⅞ of an inch deep.
Courtesy the Board of General Purposes, Freemasons' Hall.
This box and its subject are fully examined and analysed in chapter three under the heading of 'Freemasonic Boxes'.

Right
Victorian shaped rectangular snuffbox: the lid partially gilt and enriched with appliqué enamel insignia of the Masonic Order of the Knights Templar on crossed swords, and surmounted by a knight's helm. With scrolling foliage enrichment around the rim.
Maker: George Unite, Birmingham, 1894.
Size: 2½ inches by 2⅜ inches by ¾ of an inch deep.
Courtesy of the Board of General Purposes, Freemasons' Hall.

Victorian large rectangular snuffbox: with cast foliate borders, and enriched with engine-turning of the 'basketweave' motif on the lid, sides and base. Engraved in centre of lid with presentation inscription and Masonic subjects: 'compasses and squares' in all four corners.
Maker: Edward Edwards, London 1843.
Size: 4 inches by 2⅝ inches by ¾ of an inch deep.
Courtesy the Board of General Purposes, Freemasons' Hall.

George IV large rectangular snuffbox: the sides and base enriched with engine-turning of the 'basketweave' motif, the rim with cast foliate motifs. The lid has inserted repoussé plaque depicting Mrs. Siddons playing Catherine of Aragon in Shakespeare's 'Henry VIII' (Act II Scene IV).

Maker: John Barber, Birmingham 1828.

Size: 3½ inches by 2¼ inches by 1 inch deep.

Sarah Siddons (1755-1831) was the sister of the great English actor John Kemble. The part of Catherine of Aragon was perhaps her most triumphant role, and the famous painter of historical subjects, George Henry Harlow (1787-1819) recorded the scene as she addresses Cardinal Wolsey while the King and the Bishops look on. The painting was copied by the noted engraver George Clint (1770-1854) and it is probable that John Barber was inspired by this. It has already been stated in the text that engravings were the probable source for many of these 'boxlid' subjects.

Opposite page:

Upper left

Victorian large rectangular vinaigrette: silver-gilt, with inserted repoussé plaque. Subject: York Minster from the south-east, struck in high relief. The lid enriched with cast foliate rim and with engine-turning of the 'basket-weave' motif on sides and base.
Maker: Nathaniel Mills **ii**, Birmingham 1841.
Size: 1⅞ inches by 1¼ inches

Upper right

Victorian shaped rectangular vinaigrette: silver-gilt, with inserted repoussé plaque. Subject: St. Paul's Cathedral from the south-west, struck in high relief, the sides and base engraved with scrolling foliate motifs.
Maker: Nathaniel Mills **ii**, Birmingham 1852.
Size: 1¾ inches by 1¼ inches.
As has been stated in the text, Mills retired from silversmithing *circa* 1855, so this specimen is one of the last from his workshop.

Below

Victorian large rectangular snuffbox: the lid with inserted repoussé plaque. Subject: 'The Houses of Parliament'. The plaque set in heavy repoussé floral frame, the sides with floral enrichment.
Maker: Edward Smith, Birmingham 1850.
The old House of Commons was destroyed by fire in 1834, and Charles Barry (1795-1860) designed new buildings in the late Perpendicular style for the 'Mother of Parliaments'. The building was commenced in 1840 and concluded in 1860. This view of the Commons shows the view from the river of the Terrace with the partially finished Victoria Tower at the far left (it was finally completed in 1860). The tower at the far right is the unfinished clock tower which now houses 'Big Ben', the 13½ ton bell which was cast in 1856.

Centre

George IV large oval elliptical vinaigrette: silver-gilt, with cast-top. Subject: A Pair of Wading Birds, the base concentrically engine-turned with 'barleycorn' motifs, and with cast foliate border.
Makers: Ledsam, Vale & Wheeler, Birmingham 1829.
Size: 2 inches by 1⅜ inches.
Georgian cast-top subjects are uncommon.

Lower left

Victorian large rectangular vinaigrette: the lid with inserted repoussé plaque. Subject: St. George's Hall, Liverpool. Struck in high relief, and with cast foliate border.
Maker: Edward Smith, Birmingham 1854.
Size: 1½ inches by 1⅜ inches.
St. George's Hall, Liverpool was designed by Harvey Lonsdale Elmes (1815-47), and according to Sir Banister Fletcher's *magnum opus: History of Architecture on the Comparative Method*, is 'the most perfect design of the Classic School, the great hall based on the tepidarium of the Thermae of Caracalla, Rome, while externally a colonnade design is handled with great effect. Professor Cockerell (Charles Robert Cockerell, 1788-1863) completed the decoration of the interior (A.D. 1854)'. This view of St. George's Hall, is the rarest 'public building' view ever noted, and its identification made possible only through pure chance during the researches on the Houses of Parliament.

Lower right

George IV large rectangular vinaigrette: silver-gilt, the lid enriched with cast foliate scrolls and with foliate border, the sides incurving, and the base with similar cast motifs.
Maker: Edward Smith, Birmingham 1827.
Size: 1½ inches by 1 inch.

On reflection, Matthew Linwood's use of this form of 'mechanical ornament' is entirely natural: such great interest was shown in the Hero of Trafalgar and his great and victorious Battle, that any memento was eagerly sought. Linwood, or his engraver (the latter is the more likely to have introduced him to this early form of 'mass-production') had to resort to this method of keeping pace with the flood of orders, once the motif was introduced, and the temptation to 'strike while the iron was hot' (in more senses than one) must have been overpowering. The motif was accordingly 'die-struck' on a flat surface and subsequently fashioned into the lid, and then 'touched-up' by hand to give it the authentic 'hand-produced' appearance.

Another later type of 'die-stamping' was produced by Mills and his contemporaries, examples of which are shown, one of which is by George Unite, dated 1845. The subject is a presently unidentified view, possibly the Barracks at Windsor Castle with the Round Tower in the background. This variety was produced in much the same manner as Linwood's earlier specimens, with the exception that the detail—being architectural in content—is far vaguer, but also shows signs of 'touching-up' by hand. Another famous 'die-stamped' variety is the Mills' version of 'The Crystal Palace' issued in 1851, but this type is more

complex: the delicate and very effective 'raying' background was first engine-turned in a radial form, and then the design was stamped on. This variation is almost always seen on 'architectural motif' subjects, so perhaps it was found to be most effective, when used in this context.

Finally, the very last method of 'Applied Ornament' is reached. As has been hinted above, this is, perhaps, the most revolutionary of any of the devices examined. To obtain the best effect the silversmiths—Mills, Willmore, Unite and Taylor & Perry are among makers working in this medium—placed the 'acid-etched' illustration within a cartouche of real 'hand-engraved' motifs, usually floral, and somewhat coarsely executed, or, as in the instance of the Willmore subject 'The Good Samaritan' illustrated, within a heavily enriched repoussé appliqué border. The artistic intent is obviously the same: to heighten the effect of the lightly etched plaques by placing them in elaborately conceived 'frames'.

As a well-known 19th century source put it: 'In the earlier part of this century etching was a defunct art, *except as it was employed by engravers to get faster through their work, of which 'engraving' got all the credit*, the public being unable to distinguish between etched lines and lines cut with the 'burin' (a special tool for cutting on copper)'. As with 'die-stamping', the process was not a new invention: many great painters used it as a variation of their work, and Rembrandt and Van Dyck stand out as masters of their craft. Etching was particularly successful where *chiaroscuro* effects were required. P. G. Hamerton in *The Etcher's Handbook*, defined the qualities of a successful etcher thus: 'I would ask the reader to think of etching simply as a kind of highly concentrated drawing . . . the first step towards becoming an etcher is to become a good draughtsman with any kind of pointed instrument. The second step is to master the relations of light and dark in nature. The third and final stage of an etcher's

8. Acid-Etching

education is to obtain a technical mastery over copper so as to make the copper yield the precise tone he requires, whether in the space of a single line or in the shading of a space'.

Singer and Strang's classic textbook *On Etching* contains an interesting view: 'Line engraving was learned from the goldsmiths (the early goldsmiths made 'nielli', or silver plaques engraved with a 'burin' to be set in shrines, small coffers, etc, for decoration; these were then filled with a black alloy of silver, copper and lead) and etching from the armourers. The practice of ornamenting guns and arms with etched ornaments is a good deal prior to the oldest printed etching that we have been able to find'.

Two pre-19th century examples of acid-etched ornament on silver have been observed. The first, one of the exhibits at the 1952 British Antique Dealers' Fair, was an oval Charles II tobacco box dated 1682. On the apparently 'hand-engraved' lid, it bore the Arms of King, County Devon, and on the base was an acknowledged (by the exhibitor) etching of the painting 'The Money-lenders'. The Arms here, on closer examination, greatly resembled the Victorian acid-etchings, both in their elaborate attention to detail (the scrolling foliate manteling was particularly fine) and the quality of the 'shading', the subtlety of which by far exceeds anything which could be accomplished by the 'burin'. The etching on the base is far cruder in execution, and though the two subjects might not have come from the same hand, there is no reason to doubt that the acid-etching method was not applied to both.

On mature reflection, it is possible that the superbly 'engraved' oval tobacco box which appeared in *Investing in Silver* (facing page 19) in which the subject was Archbishop Sancroft, and which was, by implication, attributed to the hand of Simon Gribelin, could also be an acid-etching, as Gribelin is known to have worked in the medium for his engraved plates. The intention here, of course was not 'mass-production', but quality of delineation: by the use of an engraved copper plate, bitten by acids, a much more dramatic effect could be obtained, as well as, perhaps, that elusive 'depth' for which all engravers appear to have striven, than could be achieved with hand-engraving.

The second example is even more interesting. It is illustrated in the May, 1938 issue of *The Connoisseur*, where a brilliantly 'engraved' oval tea-caddy by Andrew Fogelberg, London, 1772, appears. The editorial comments 'Its execution is exceptional for a piece of silver, on which as a rule the conventional character of the ornament requires a somewhat heavy and even incision. This, however, is cut in lines of extraordinary fineness, showing a much more delicate tool has been employed. In addition to the difference in execution as compared to the usual ornamentation of silver, the design itself is a noteworthy one, and is so reminiscent of Morland, with its group around the inn door (the engraving shows an innkeeper proffering a tankard to an obviously inebriated gentleman, while a lady tries to restrain the latter from accepting it) that it is baffling to find an origin for it at a time when the great *genre* painter was only nine years old (he was born in 1703). The whole has the appearance of an *etched plate, designed and executed by the same hand*.' After a full description of the subject, the editorial probes the possible identity of the artist who was also an etcher fine enough to have accomplished this fine piece of enrichment, and suggests the Alsatian artist, Philippe Jacques de Loutherbourg, who came from Paris to London in 1771, became an A.R.A. in 1780 and an R.A. in 1781.

On close examination, under a strong glass, the 'engraving' on the tea-caddy is indeed etched. The italics and parentheses are those of the present writer.

To return to the Birmingham 'acid-etching' period: two patents associated with the process were granted within the first half of the 19th century. The first was issued to John Ham, Vinegar Maker, of Bristol in December 1826, for 'An improved process for promoting the actions of the Acetic Acid on metallic bodies'. The invention primarily consisted of improved cisterns for the acid vapours to circulate 'by presenting an extensive surface to the atmospheric air, so that the acidification of the vineous fluid, and the corrosion and solution of the metal shall proceed simultaneously'.

The second patent was granted to Charles Hullmandel, lithographic printer of London, in September 1838 and consisted of 'A new mode of preparing certain surfaces for being corroded with acids in order to produce patterns and designs for the purposes of certain kinds of printing and transparencies'. The specification in this instance consisted of improved methods of preparing the 'mordant', that is, the fluid used to 'bite in' the lines, to Mr. Hullmandel's own recipe, and in preparing the surfaces to accept this, by means of various gums and the 'best lamp black'. This last is a pigment consisting of almost pure carbon in a state of

fine division, made by collecting the soot produced by burning oil; an early mention of the process occurred in Henry Peacham's *The Gentleman's Exercise*, 1612, speaking of the 'art of drawing and limming [sic]': 'The making of ordinary lamp blacke. Take a torch or linke, and hold it vnder the bottom of a latten basen, and as it groweth to be furd and blacke within, strike it with a feather into some shell or other, and grinde it with gumme-water'. The Birmingham engraver who was instrumental in uncovering this process, also stated that the Victorian 'acid-etchings' were produced with wax and lamp-black.

Bearing all the above in mind, namely, that patented inventions (as well, perhaps, as trade secrets of the older methods) were available at the time that the first 'acid-etched' boxes appeared—the earliest observed was dated 1830—it is no longer surprising that craftsmen of Mills' calibre did not hesitate to use the method to embellish some of their finest boxes. Far from detracting from their value, (as has already been stated above, in the preamble to this long survey on 'Applied Ornament') the process would appear to have enhanced these fine *objets d'art*: any clever silversmith could employ an engraver, but who would have thought that corrosive elements could produce such beautiful effects with pictures and designs?

Victorian cheroot case: of rectangular form with rounded corners. Acid-etched with 'hunting-scene' on lid, set in hand-engraved scrolling foliate motifs. 'Integral-hinge', and with 'push-piece' opener.
Maker: Nathaniel Mills **ii**, Birmingham 1855.
Size: 6 inches by 3½ inches by 1 inch deep.
This article was made in Mills' last years but lacks nothing in beauty of design.

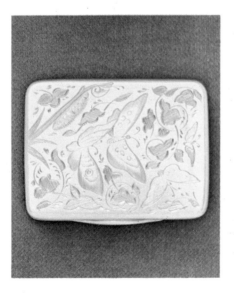

Victorian 'acid-etched' rectangular vinaigrette: the lid embellished with superb 'love-birds' motif, the base with 'butterflies and foliage' motif. Applied vertically on lid. Slightly projecting thumbpiece.
Maker: Charles H. Cheshire, Birmingham 1878.
Size: 1⅜ inches by 1 inch.
Charles H. Cheshire worked at Birmingham from 1867 to 1907; his mark is entered at the Birmingham Assay Office.

Postscript

No examination of 'Applied Ornament' could be considered complete without some mention of three aspects, which have been deliberately left to the very end of the chapter. The first of these is a brief history of snuff boxes and vinaigrettes: Nothing has been said so far about the introduction of either tobacco or snuff into England, as this very subject received careful and complete scrutiny in *Investing in Silver*, but it is possible that some readers might not have had the opportunity, or the desire to read this work. In order, therefore, to ensure that nothing salient is missed out from an otherwise overall survey, the following short history is appended:

The tobacco plant was brought to Europe in 1558 by Francisco Fernandes, a physician who had been sent by Philip II of Spain to investigate the products of Mexico. The French ambassador to Portugal sent seeds of the plant to the Queen, Catherine de Medici, and thereby immortalised himself—his name was Jean Nicot—and Ralph Lane, the first governor of Virginia, and Sir Walter Raleigh brought with them, on their return from the newly settled English possession in 1586, the implements and materials of tobacco-smoking. The habit soon spread all over England, and in 1604 King James I attempted to stem it by placing a crippling tax of six shillings and tenpence per pound upon the tobacco, which had, until that time, been taxed at *two-pence* per pound. This tax, besides being extremely unpopular, had no other appreciable effects, beyond driving the smokers under cover, until the beginning of the Commonwealth. So popular did tobacco become, that from the earliest times, both pipes and boxes were made in precious metals. The earliest tobacco box noted was dated 1643 and was of the oval 'lift-off' lid variety, and a silver pipe has been recently discovered which, though undated, could, from its early style, also date from about that time. It has a pleasantly curving stem, which can be removed from the bowl, and the latter is very small, not much larger than the diameter of a man's little

William IV acid-etched snuff box: subject: 'The Good Samaritan'. Set in heavy foliate and scroll border and with foliate thumbpiece. Maker: Joseph Willmore, Birmingham, 1832. *Courtesy of the Birmingham Assay Office.*

finger. There is a ball-shaped 'saliva-cup' on the stem, near the union with the bowl and it is about nine inches in length.

An unusual term for a snuff box has been noted: this appears in *Hoare's Bank: A Record* 1673-1932, which was published to commemorate the opening of a new branch in London's West End by that illustrious business house, In the account book of Richard Hoare, the founder of the Bank, who was also a notable goldsmith, appears the following entry for 'May ye 18th 1694': For a *snush Box* Double Covered over with Shagreene wtt 2 oz. 7 dwt. att £3 00 0'. This term 'snush' is found in the Gloucestershire dialect and also in Highland and Gaelic. The English poet, Matthew Prior (1664–1721) writing in his *Cupid and Ganymede*, 1709, versifies thus: 'A snush-box, set with bleeding hearts, rubies, all pierced with diamond darts', and the *London Gazette* for 1682 lists a 'round gold Snushbox' which had been stolen or lost.

The English Vinaigrette was the natural successor to the earlier pomander, of which much has been written above. As far as may be ascertained, the type originated in the late 1750's, but it was not until the 1790's that it became universally admired and thus produced in many forms and shapes. The early boxes were simple containers with crudely pierced protective 'grilles' but as the 19th century arrived, a whole wealth of fascinating shapes were created by the clever silversmiths. In this trade, the Birmingham craftsmen, in particular, were extremely active. Basically, the box is a container for an acetic acid-soaked sponge, which served as a 'reviver' and stimulant, and was popular with both sexes. Aromatics were introduced to make the acid more pleasant to the smell, and, in order to prevent the astringent acid from splashing onto the skin and clothes, the protective 'grille' with all its charming embellishment was inserted.

As will be noted, the final chapter in this work is entirely devoted to the biographies of five famous Birmingham silversmiths. It is therefore necessary to

Upper left
George III vinaigrette: small rectangular, set with mother-of-pearl plaque in lid.
Makers: Wardell & Kempston, Birmingham, 1812.
Courtesy of the Birmingham Assay Office.

Upper right
George III vinaigrette: circular, cast concentric motif on lid and base, formed as a 'watch'.
Maker: Samuel Pemberton **vi**, Birmingham 1808.
Courtesy of the Birmingham Assay Office.

Lower left
Victorian large vinaigrette: shaped rectangular parcel-gilt (partially gilt), the lid engraved with the Coat-of-Arms of Chandos, the 1st Baron Leigh. Barony created 11th May, 1839. Born 1791, died 1850.
Maker: Nathaniel Mills **ii**, Birmingham 1841.
Size: 2½ inches by 1⅝ inches.
Courtesy of the Birmingham Assay Office.

Lower right
George III vinaigrette: rectangular cast-top, silver-gilt.
Subject: 'Hare in Reeds' designed by Thomas Bewick.
Maker: Thomas Newbold, Birmingham 1820.
Grille pierced with 'Greek Key' motif.
Courtesy of the Birmingham Assay Office.

Victorian 'cartouche-shaped' vinaigrette: enriched with 'barleycorn' motif engine-turning, with cast foliate thumbpiece, and 'standaway' hinge. The hand-pierced floral grille opens upwards.
Maker: William Simpson, Birmingham 1840.
Size: 1½ inches by 1 inch by ¼ of an inch deep. William Simpson entered his mark at Birmingham in 1825.

Upper right
George III cast-top rectangular vinaigrette: formed as a silver-gilt wallet, with floral bright-cutting on the 'flap' and 'scale-motif' engraving on the lid. With 'die-stamped' filigree grille.
Maker: Matthew Linwood **v**, Birmingham 1816.
Struck between the lion passant and the maker's mark, is the figure '2', so Linwood probably had a team of workers making the vinaigrettes, as this a 'workers' punch'.
Size 1¾ inches by 1⅛ inches.

Below
George III hand-engraved vinaigrette: the lid with vertical 'Nursery Rhymes' theme: subject: 'Little Boy Blue'. With finely 'die-stamped' 'basket of flowers' grille.
Maker: Matthew Linwood **v**, Birmingham, 1808.
Size: 1 inch by ⅞ of an inch.

cite something of the metropolitan makers, in order that the record be kept straight. Of the many fine boxes illustrated, about half are by London makers, most of whose marks appear in Jackson. Where, in the captions, details are given which are not in that work, these have been obtained from the Register of Makers at Goldsmiths' Hall, London, where four marks which are not in Jackson have been noted; as all are of the early 18th century, it might be of interest to cite them here:

Br and EB: The two marks of Erick Brandt, snuffbox maker, who worked in St. Martin's le Grand and entered his mark at Goldsmiths' Hall on May 24th, 1729.

GM in a rectangle and GM in a Shield: The first and second marks of George Moreland, snuffbox maker, who worked in Maiden Lane at the time when he entered his second mark at Goldsmiths' Hall on the 30th June, 1731. His first entry was in 1723.

IW in an oval: John Wingler, snuffbox maker, who worked at Cock Pit Court, Jewell Street, and entered his mark at Goldsmiths' Hall on the 6th of April, 1738.

RW in an incused rectangle: Richard Weaver, snuffbox maker who worked at Addle Hill, near Doctors Commons, and entered his mark on the 4th of May, 1738.

Something should also be said about Samson Mordan, whose delightful 'confections' appear in vinaigrette form from about 1840. He was a skilled engineer and inventor, and patented the first propelling pencil in 1822. He was born *circa* 1781 and died in 1870. In 1850 his business premises were at 22 City Road, and the firm carried on in business until 1940 at 41 City Road, when the premises were bombed, and the employees absorbed by another firm.

4. The Birmingham Boxmakers

Upper left
George III vinaigrette grille: showing 'National Emblems'—Rose, Thistle and Shamrock.
Maker: Matthew Linwood **v**, Birmingham 1812.
Size: 1 inch by ¾ of an inch.

Upper right
George III vinaigrette grille: subject: a pair of lovebirds in a hand-pierced foliate frame.
Makers: Lawrence & Company, Birmingham 1818.
Size: 1½ inches by 1 inch.

Lower left
George IV vinaigrette grille: subject: Phoenix in a hand-pierced scrolling foliate frame.
Maker: James William Garland, London 1828.

Size: 1½ inches by 1 inch.
Garland's mark **IWG** was entered at Goldsmiths' Hall in August, 1826, when he was working at 16 Bridgewater Street, off Aldersgate Street.

Lower right
Victorian vinaigrette grille: subject: 'crossed quills and a book' in hand-pieced foliage.
Maker: Edward Edwards, London 1846.
Size: 1½ inches by 1 inch.

Until 1923, when Major-General R. C. B. Pemberton's monumental *Pemberton Pedigrees* appeared, it was generally believed that there were no silversmiths working in Birmingham until the middle of the 18th century. General Pemberton's massive and overwhelmingly profuse research of all the various branches of the Family, in Europe, America, Canada, and New Zealand, opened up new fields for historians, and certainly, it has made the task of tracing the background of at least one Birmingham silversmithing family a great deal easier for the present writer. Full details of this study will appear below.

In an article, learned as always, by the late Edward Alfred Jones, which appeared in *Apollo Magazine* in February, 1944, entitled *Some English Provincial Goldsmiths*, the author, basing his work on one of the genealogies contained in *Pemberton Pedigrees*, and on information supplied by the then Birmingham City Librarian, Mr. H. M. Cashmore, stated the following: 'ROGER PEMBERTON, goldsmith, died in 1628. His son, Thomas (1589–1640), also a goldsmith, in his will dated and proved 1640, wished to be buried at the upper end of the "Maisters Chauncell" in the Parish Church of Birmingham, and desired that his son, Thomas, should "serve and dwell an apprentice with his mother for term of 8 years in the trade of a goldsmith". He left her £50 worth of plate "most necessary for furnishing the said trade", and all his tools to his said son (1624–93) who was a goldsmith and ironmonger of Bennett's Hill'.

It will be seen, therefore, that some sort of minor industry in the working of precious metals existed in the city long before Birmingham became nationally famous for the excellence of its wares, thanks largely to Matthew Boulton's determined stand over the establishment of its own Assay Office, which aim, when realised in 1773, organised the industry into a prosperous and healthy body. It needs to be stressed, however, that Birmingham had long been a producer of base-metal wares, chiefly iron and brass, and the late Arthur Westwood, Esq., Assay Master of Birmingham in the early part of this century, read a very learned and important paper to the *Birmingham Archaeological Society* in March 1904, in which the following interesting statement appeared: 'The traveller Misson (a French Huguenot lawyer who became a travelling tutor and journeyed through Italy, and died in London in 1721) visiting Milan towards the end of the 17th century, speaks of the fine works of rock crystal, swords, heads of canes, snuffboxes, and other fine 'works of Steel' he saw there, but remarks that "they can be had cheaper and better at Birmingham"'. It should be added that this masterly paper with its mass of valuable data has been the 'spur' which initiated the present writer's interest in the old Birmingham craftsmen, and finally prompted his investigations into the genealogies of the five craftsmen, namely, Samuel Pemberton, Matthew Linwood, Joseph Willmore, Joseph Taylor and Nathaniel Mills.

Before these are undertaken, it is imperative that some mention at least, be made of the two progenitors of the Birmingham Silver Trade—Matthew Boulton and James Watt—the celebrated industrialist on the one hand, and the inventive genius on the other, through whose combined business acumen and engineering prowess Birmingham became the centre of a large manufacturing empire. Boulton was born in Birmingham in 1728. On his father's death in 1759, he inherited the family metal manufacturing business, and in 1764 removed the works from Snow Hill to a much larger area at Soho in the north of the city. Here, he manufactured various 'toys', and as Dr. Erasmus Darwin, the famous physician and man of letters wrote in 1768 'Here are toys and utensils of various kinds, in gold, copper, tortoiseshell, enamels, and many vitreous and metallic compositions, with gilt, plated, and inlaid works, all wrought up to the finest elegance and perfection of execution'.

Matthew Boulton was an adventurous trader, and in 1765, began to manufacture solid silver plate in association with John Fothergill, and in 1778–80 to reproduce oil paintings by a mechanical process in association with Francis Eginton (1737–1805, see above). Both ventures, however, were doomed to failure. As H. W. Dickinson says, in his absorbing work *Matthew Boulton*, 'The partnership of Boulton and Fothergill was an unsuccessful one. From a statement prepared by Zaccaeus Walker, the clerk to the firm, it appears that on a capital of £20,000, the excess of losses over profits for the eighteen years of the partnership ending 1780 was upwards of £11,000. Had it not been for the sales of his wives' estates (Boulton married twice, first Mary Robinson, and secondly his deceased wife's sister, Anne, whose combined fortunes he inherited) the firm must inevitably have gone bankrupt, because the profits from the steam engine business had not yet materialised'.

Boulton was not, it would appear, an actual silversmith himself, but the driving force behind the scenes of a busy, progressive, and thriving enterprise. The masterpieces bearing his famous mark—in association with John Fothergill he headed the entries in the first Register of the newly founded Assay Office in 1773—were produced by the many craftsmen and apprentices whom he attracted to his great 'Soho Works'. Very little is known about the identity of these apprentices, but two names stand out as famous artists in their own right. John Gregory Hancock, the noted engraver and die-sinker, mentioned above in relation to his patent for 'die-stamping' designs on metal, was apprenticed to Boulton in 1766. He was the son of the renowned engraver of Battersea Enamels and Worcester Porcelain, Robert Hancock.

As was mentioned above, *inter alia*, Edward Thomason was another Boulton apprentice. He commenced work with him at the age of 16 remaining at Soho until he was 21 years old. In 1793, he started in business on his own and eventually produced gilt and plated buttons, jewellery, medals and tokens, and later, silver plate. Next to Soho, his premises in Church Street (very near his Master's) were the largest in Birmingham. An advertisement of 1830 is illuminating for the detailed list of the items produced, and is of interest at the present juncture because it provides the reader with a good insight of the stock which had to be carried by a large contemporary manufactory. It is thus given in full:

'Silver Services of all descriptions.
Plated   Do   Do   Do
Plated cutlery, Spoons &c. on Steel.
Fine Cut Glass for the Table.
Bronzed or Mulu [ormulu] Figures and Lustres
Papier Mache Trays & Cabinets
—Exclusively—
A Great Variety of Patent Articles and Mechanical Inventions—and His Majestys Royal Letters Patent for the Making of Gold and Silver Mounted Medals And Coins—The Medal Dies of the Kings—of Celebrated Men—of the Victories of the Late war—of The Elgin Marbles [brought to England in 1816]—of Science and Philosophy—of Society and other Medals. Jewellery and Gold and Silver Snuff Boxes. Brass and Bronzed Staircases.
Communion Plate, Cups and Vases in Gold and Silver'.

Edward Thomason entered his first mark in 1809–10, was a leading figure in Birmingham commerce, the Vice-Consul for Russia, France, Prussia, Austria, Spain, Portugal, Brazils, Sweden and Norway, and held the Knighthood of nine countries, including Great Britain, the latter being granted to him in 1832. He married Phyllis Bown Glover, the daughter of Samuel Glover of Abercarne, near Newport. Monmouthshire, and had one son, Henry Botfield, who died in 1843, aged 41. The 'John Thomason' who partnered John Hilliard, and whose joint mark was 'H & T', entered at the Assay Office in 1847, might have been a nephew, the son of Sir Edward's brother James. This latter partnership, according to Jackson, was still active in 1882. Sir Edward retired from business in 1835, wrote his memoirs in two volumes in 1845, and died in May 1849.

Matthew Boulton's partnership with James Watt (as opposed to that with John Fothergill) was blessed with success. Watt, born at Greenock in 1736, the son of a merchant and town-councillor, came to Glasgow in 1754 to learn the trade of a mathematical-instrument maker, and set up in business there. As early as 1759, his attention had been directed to steam as a motive-force, and he made a series of experiments, which, however, led to no positive results. In 1763, while he was working at Glasgow University, a working model of Thomas Newcomen's Engine (adapted by Newcomen before 1698 from an earlier engine by a Captain

Savery) was sent for repair from a college class-room. Watt soon repaired it, and, on seeing the defects in the design of the machine, made a number of improvements. Watt's great invention, which revolutionised the production of cheap steam-driven power, and brought eventual prosperity to Birmingham was, according to Dickinson 'to instal a separate condenser. The effect of this was a saving of from two thirds to three quarters of the coal, as compared with the old engine doing the same work'.

The remainder of Watt's life-story is one of success, and he died at Heathfield Hall, his seat near Birmingham in 1819. In 1824, his Memorial was erected in Handsworth Church, where he is buried, at a cost of £2,000, which was raised by public subscription. The sculptor was the great 19th century artist Sir Francis Legatt Chantrey, and the great inventor is shown seated, in thoughtful mien, contemplating a plan. This very fine sculpture was copied by the Mills workshop in 1838, and appears on the superb vertical lid snuffbox illustrated. The quality of the casting is absolutely supreme, and the original model must have been carved by a master-craftsman. The box is Number One in the Birmingham Assay Office Collection, and is justly admired. It is the apotheosis of the Silversmith's craft.

Matthew Boulton's enterprises were very widespread. According to Dickinson, he had no fewer than thirteen different businesses between 1759 and 1809, including Plated and Silver ware, Steam Engines, Buttons, Medals, the Mint for government copper coins and an Iron Foundry. His biographer leaves us with this picture of him: 'In appearance Boulton was above the medium height with a fine figure and erect carriage. He had a handsome face, with somewhat receding forehead, a firm chin and grey eyes with a humorous twinkle in them under well-arched eyebrows. Boulton's manners were charming and easy as if accustomed to wealth and habitual command. Doubtless this arose from his intercourse with persons in high places in a period when manners certainly were polished. This address secured for him entrée to the very highest in the land. Boulton was always well dressed, and we must not forget what an addition to a man's appearance was afforded by the picturesque dress of the period: the grey peruke, the embroidered coat, set off with some of his own buttons, the lace jabot and lace at the wrists, the flowered waistcoat, the knee-breeches, the silk stockings, the inlaid buckles, again his own, on the polished shoes; we even hear, on one occasion, of his wearing a sword'.

Boulton died on the 17th of August, 1809 in the eighty-first year of his age. The funeral was attended by thousands of people. The cortege was followed by a procession of 600 workmen from the Manufactory and Foundry, and a Memorial Medal, in copper, was presented to each individual invited to attend the funeral, which, on the obverse read: 'Matthew Boulton, died August 17th, 1809 aged 81 years', and on the reverse, in a palm-wreath, the words: 'In memory of his obsequies August 24th, 1809'.

Having thus set the scene for a genealogical survey of the Birmingham boxmakers, something should be said of the writer's research programme and his aims in general. As far as may be presently ascertained, with the solitary exception of the Pemberton Tables, no other biographies of the above-mentioned silversmiths exist, and consequently no bibliographical material. Feeling this anomaly to be unjust in view of the great mastery which these master-craftsmen attained over their medium, and of the adulation which other eminent figures in the Craft have received through their published biographies, the writer set himself the task of tracing at least something of their history.

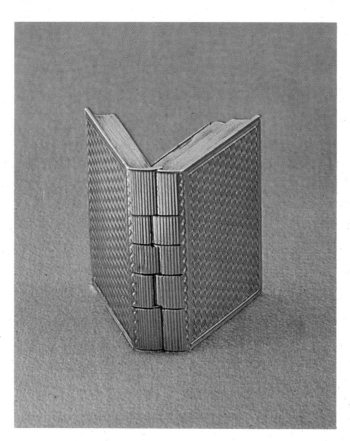

George III silver-gilt shaped vinaigrette: formed as a superlatively designed book. The sides finely engine-turned with 'basketweave' motifs, the 'edges' finely enriched with 'thread scoring' motifs, and the hinge of the finest possible conception of a refined 'tenon and mortise' variety.
Maker: John Reilly, London 1809.
Size: 1¼ inches by 1 inch.

Victorian shaped vinaigrette: formed as a 'Policeman's Lamp', the conical lid with 'clasp' lifts up to reveal the grille. With 'simulated spherical reflector' and suspensory loop.
Maker: Samson Mordan, London 1877.
Size: 2½ inches by ⅞ of an inch in diameter.

Opposite
Pair 'presently unique' silver-gilt vinaigrettes:

formed as silver-gilt veined leaves (possibly birch). Both by Joseph Willmore, Birmingham but dated 1825 and 1831 respectively. Of shallow form and with 'wire-loop' handles, and 'integral' three-lugged hinges. There are no grilles—the sponge being held in position by a wire frame—and the marks are on the loop-handles.
Size: 1½ inches.
Courtesy of the Birmingham Assay Office.

Victorian finely cast 'Tiger's Head' vinaigrette the jaws and fangs superbly delineated, the vinaigrette being formed of the inside of the head, with simply pierced floral grille. The circular lid set with bloodstone, and the head has suspensory loop.
Maker: Samson Morden, London, 1860.
Size: 1 inch by ¾ of an inch.
Mordan's vinaigrettes are seldom marked with more than the Maker's mark and, occasionally, with the mid-Victorian 'Registry Marks' which consist of a 'diamond-shaped' lozenge surmounted by a sphere, these containing various coded figures and letters. Thus, both the month and year of manufacture are given, although not in the familiar Assay Office form. This table can be found in Patricia Wardle's interesting survey of *Victorian Silver and Silver-plate* (pages 225-6).

Over page: Upper left
William IV shaped vinaigrette: formed as a walnut. Of cast and chased form simulating the natural fruit. Florally pierced hinged grille.
Makers: Taylor and Perry, Birmingham 1834.
Size: 2 inches by 1½ inches.

Upper right
William IV shaped vinaigrette: formed as reclining cow. The flat base with 'integral-hinge', and hinged florally pierced grille.
Makers: Wilkinson and Company, Sheffield 1834.
Size: 2 inches by 1 inch by 1 inch deep.
This article is fully marked on the base and partially marked on the grille, otherwise the suspicion might arise that it was made from a terminal of an Irish butter-dish.

Centre left
George IV shaped vinaigrette: formed as a 'beehive'. The tubular container with die-struck concentric rings and domed pull-off lid. Pull-out grille.
Maker: Thomas Willmore, Birmingham 1822.
Size: 1¼ inches by ¾ of an inch in diameter.

Centre right
Victorian shaped vinaigrette: formed as a 'cane-top'. The knob of octagonal shape, and with 'integral-hinged' domed lid. Engraved with foliate motifs, and with simply pierced floral grille.
Unmarked, *circa* 1850.
Size: 1½ by 1¼ inches in diameter.

Lower left
George III 'lion-shaped' snuffbox: depicting 'couchant lion' of fierce countenance with well modelled mane. Flat hinged base and the tail forming the handle.
Maker: George Ashworth and Company, Sheffield 1812.
Size: 2½ inches by 1⅜ inches.
According to the Sheffield City Museum, there are very few Sheffield-made boxes.

Lower right
George III shaped vinaigrette: formed as a 'fish', the lid and base hand-engraved with 'scale' motifs, the projecting fins forming the thumbpieces, and with 'stand-away' hinge. The grille also of 'piscatorial' form. With suspensory loop at mouth.
Maker: Joseph Taylor, Birmingham 1818.
Size: 1½ inches by ½ an inch.

This was accomplished, in the first instance, through a massive search of the Birmingham Trade Directories dating from 1767 to 1840, and to contemporary newspaper obituaries. The latter, however, yielded little, as unlike the death appreciations of today, the 18th and 19th century obituaries contained very little biographical details. This was followed by a period of intensive study of church records, both in Birmingham and London, to determine the places of interment of the five families, as additional data could be gleaned from memorials and tombstones. Again, it will be noted that this stratagem was only partially successful. The 'A' Register of the Birmingham Assay Office (that is, the first Register opened when the Office was created in 1773) ceded valuable information on all the makers researched, and enlargements of the various makers' marks will be found interspersed with the biographies, thereby illustrating the various epochs of the firms, and revealing partners and successors.

As was stated above, Major-General Pemberton's *Pemberton Pedigrees* contains the complete genealogical history of this illustrious family, and thus, in but one instance, the research was entirely simplified. So many details appear, as to make the other family histories very sparse indeed, but it is probable that the Pembertons' links with the aristocracy (of which, more later) resulted in the existence of so much contemporary data, although, of course, this is not to denigrate General Pemberton's wonderful achievement; his researches must have been exceptionally difficult (they always are, for a pioneer) and occupied many years of devoted study before they came to final fruition. The remaining four families, namely, Linwood, Taylor, Willmore and Mills, who were selected for study because they, and the Pembertons are among the elite of the Birmingham Boxmakers, came from yeoman stock,

and while a certain amount of genealogical information concerning the Linwoods (or *Lynwood*, as they appear in the early records) is available, primarily due to the fact that they claimed to be Lords of the Manor of the village of Cogenhoe, near Northampton, and because their lineage goes back to the early part of the 17th century, nothing at all is known of either the Willmore, Taylor or Mills families beyond the late 18th century.

It has not been possible, for instance, to trace many personal accounts of these and of the few poignant touches in this otherwise wholly impersonal survey, the death from Scarlatina, of the two youngest sons of Nathaniel Mills, Junior, in 1848, within two days of each other, stands out. Their little marble tombstone is in Key Hill Cemetery, near their home and the family's workshop, but only the vault number identifies their last resting place, as their names have been erased by the elements. Similarly, Mary Anne, the wife of Joseph Willmore, died in childbirth in 1848 at the age of 40. Otherwise little more is known of their personal lives.

Again, while the history of the Pembertons is so well documented nothing personal has emerged, beyond one solitary incident, the veracity of which is, however, debatable. It is cited by Thomas De Quincey in his *Literary Reminiscences and Conversations with Woodhouse* (appended to the Parchment Series Edition of *The English Opium Eater*. According to this account, Charles Lloyd, the poet and friend of Samuel Coleridge and Charles Lamb, and son of Charles Lloyd of the famous banking family of Birmingham, threatened to elope with Sophia, the third daughter of Samuel Pemberton *the fourth* (the italicised appellation will be explained below), when he was 23 and she was 20 in 1799. It is not certain that they did elope, although they were married in that year. Sophia died at Versailles in 1830, and Lloyd expired in a French lunatic asylum in 1839.

The Pembertons

It has already been explained that this particular genealogy is based on General Pemberton's *Pemberton Pedigrees*. Speaking of Charts 17–25, which contain the genealogical tables of the Birmingham families (other branches are found in Lancashire and Cheshire, Northampton and St. Albans) the General says: 'All the Pemberton families of Birmingham itself, with one exception, are descended from Roger Pemberton, who was Mayor of Walsall in 1509, and who, in turn, could probably trace his descent from one Thurstan de Pemberton, who married Emma de Winstanley, at Lichfield in 1417'. His son, Roger, has already been mentioned above. These early Pembertons number three goldsmiths in their ranks: Roger **iii** (married 1584, died 1628), his son Thomas **v** (*vide supra*) (1589–1640), and his grandson, Thomas **vi** of Bennett's Hill (1624–1693), the 'ironmonger and goldsmith'.

The Founder of the branch which contained the 'Samuels' (that is, the silversmiths whose genealogies are here investigated) was Nathaniel **ii** (1634–1687), the son of Thomas **v**. He was a cutler to whom was born, in 1668 Samuel **ii**. The latter was married to Elizabeth Mason in 1702, and died *circa* 1733; his trade is not given. The Samuel who founded the silversmiths' business and is designated as a 'Jeweller and Toy Maker', is Samuel **iii**, of Snow Hill, who was born in 1704 and died in 1784. His wife's surname is not given, but her Christian name was Rebecca. This Pemberton was not registered at the Assay Office.

His son, Samuel **iv** of Edgbaston and Five Ways, 'Jeweller and Toy Maker' was born *circa* 1728, and married Mary Grosvenor in 1769. He entered his mark at the Assay Office in 1773, and, as can be seen from the illustration, there were six marks altogether, of three distinct styles: one, probably the earliest, was **SP** in a rectangular punch. The others were **SP** in oval punches of various sizes, for larger and smaller plate (other articles besides boxes

1

were, of course, wrought by this workshop) and one very rare mark, **SP** in Old English Gothic lettering, which is not at all similar to Jackson's version dated 1784 in his Supplementary List of Additional Marks on page 414. The punch is of the 'cut-corner' variety, and the **P** is much more Gothicised.

This Samuel (**iv**) was the father of Sophia and of Elizabeth, who married William Ryland in 1761. The next possessor of the name was Samuel **vi** who was born in 1771, and is described as a 'Jeweller of Livery Street'. He took his son into partnership and thus the firm became known as 'Samuel Pemberton & Son of Snow Hill'. So it is probable that his retail shop was in Livery Street and the works at Snow Hill.

In 1812, one of Samuel **vi**'s apprentices, Robert Mitchell, left

 2

 3

 5   SP

him to go into business on his own (see Mark 2) but appears to have rejoined the firm in the same year as the mark **P & M** in a rectangular punch (see Mark 3) was entered and the inscription in the **'A'** Register states: 'Saml. Pemberton & Son & Mitchell'. It is probable, however, that the partner was not Samuel but his brother Thomas **xvi** of Five Ways (who was born in 1775, married Mary Frances Hooke in 1808, and died in 1830). As will be noted, the **P & M** mark (No. 3) and the joint **TP/RM** mark (entered in 1816) are joined by another **P & M** (No. 5) which is quite separate from the **SP** mark in a plain rectangular punch. A further set of marks was entered into the Register in 1821, and Thomas Pemberton's mark alone appears, so the partnership must have lapsed by then (see Mark No. 6). The **SP** struck without a cartouche is probably a watch-case mark, as the Pemberton and Mitchell partnership was entered as for 'Watch Cases &c'.

Samuel **vi** died in 1836. There are no more gold or silversmiths in the Pemberton Tables.

The General states that Thomas **vi** and his descendants were Quakers, but he does not say, possibly because it was not within his 'terms of reference', that the Quaker line died out in the mid-1750's, and that, thereafter, the silversmithing Pembertons were Nonconformists. Catherine Hutton Beale, in her *Memorials of the Old Meeting House and Burial Ground, Birmingham* (published by subscription in 1882) stated that her aim in writing the Memorials was to preserve the records of the Meeting House, which was to be demolished by virtue of an Act of Parliament, in order to enlarge New Street Station. She included a plan of the graveyard, which contained the vaults of various families, and the Chapel, in which the Pembertons occupied the Low Altar Tomb. The Memorial reads as follows:

IN MEMORY OF
SAMUEL PEMBERTON who died Aug 16th 1784 Aged 80
ALSO OF
REBECCA his Wife, who died Nov 28th 1769 aged 70
AND OF
THOMAS PEMBERTON their son, who died Nov 6th 1768 aged 27
AND OF
SAMUEL PEMBERTON their son, who died Aug 14th 1803 aged 65
AND OF
MARY GROSVENOR his wife, who died Nov 3rd 1817 aged 73
LIKEWISE OF
SAMUEL, REBECCA, LUCIANA, CAROLINE AND GEORGE
Children of SAMUEL PEMBERTON jun
and MARY his wife
Who all died young
ALSO OF
THOMAS PEMBERTON who died March 18th 1830 aged 54
AND OF
MARIA his wife who died 11th Sep 1836
ALSO OF
EDWIN PEMBERTON Born 19th July 1785 died 1st August 1851

This concludes the Pemberton Genealogy.

 6   S P

The Linwoods of Cogenhoe

The name 'Matthew Linwood' is shared by six members of the same family, and this could prove to be very confusing to the reader, so the placing of a bold Roman numeral against each 'Matthew' as it occurs, should make it possible to identify them all without difficulty. The trail which led to the uncovering of this, by no means simple genealogy, was instigated, in the first instance, by the identification of the renowned 18th century embroideress Mary Linwood, as a relative of one of the 'Matthews', and the further discovery, in a pamphlet, that she had links with a Northamptonshire family. This led to enquiries of the Northamptonshire Archives Committee, and the reply from the then Archivist, P. I. King, Esq., MA, led to researches at the Leicester Department of Archives. These revealed the existence of a massive genealogy undertaken by a great-great-great-great-grandson of Hannah Meredith (who, as will be shown below, married the founder of the silversmithing business), the late Charles Linwood, of Victoria, Australia.

This, in turn, was based in part on material taken from the Parish Registers by the Rector of Cogenhoe, the Reverend R. Dunwell. The remaining details were compiled from vigorous researches at Somerset House, the Greater London Record Office

at County Hall, and the Local Studies Library of the Birmingham Central Reference Library, and, finally, but most important of all, upon information supplied by the widow of Charles Linwood, Mrs. Beryl Linwood.

The first step, the perusal of the 'Obituary Index' of Aris's *Birmingham Gazette*, (which proved of such value in tracing the genealogy of the Mills family, below) laid nothing but a trail of 'red herrings', that is, misleading information; as has been mentioned above, contemporary obituary notices rarely gave biographical details, and thus, the entry for the 10th of August 1840 which reads: 'On the 2nd inst, at Edgbaston in his 80th year, Mr. Linwood, late of St. Paul's Square. A man universally admired and respected for his work and strict integrity both in public and private life' led to the mistaken assumption that this referred to Matthew Linwood **iv**, it being thought that he was the only member of his family to achieve eminence. In actual fact, the subject of this obituary was John, who was himself a renowned figure in Birmingham, and had a plating establishment in that city. He was baptised in 1760 and, as stated above, died in 1840, and a note of this decease appears in *The Gentleman's Magazine* of that latter year.

The 'king-pin' upon whom all the first investigations could be based, was William Linwood, Esq., of Forty Hill, Enfield, in the County of Middlesex ('William the Slave Driver', as he was known to his family) the discovery of whose will opened up new vistas of research. There are several enlightening phrases which occur in the will, such as 'to Frances Giles Linwood, wife of my late brother Matthew' and 'Hannah Linwood, daughter of my late brother John' which enabled the genealogy to be painstakingly built up. Furthermore, there is mention in the will of one 'Whaley Markland', who was appointed an executor, and is designated a nephew. According to the late Charles Linwood's 'Family Tree', Matthew **v**'s elder sister, Sarah, born in 1759, married Samuel Markland in 1798, and when it is remembered that Matthew's grandmother's maiden name was 'Whalley' or 'Whaley', the combined names point to direct links between the various persons.

The second lead came from a slim pamphlet issued by the Leicester City Museums, written by Norma L. Whitcomb, which formed an introduction to the work of Mary Linwood. It had been thought that she was a relative—probably a cousin—of Matthew **v**, but this publication contains the sentence: 'Mary Linwood was born in Birmingham in 1756, one of a *large* family, including a sister, Ann, who composed music, a brother John who invented a mechanical meatjack, and William nicknamed "The Slave Driver".' When it is remembered that Matthew **v** was one of a family of seven children, and had a brother named William, and one named John, and a sister named Ann, the conclusion that Mary Linwood's father and Matthew **v**'s father were one and the same, is inescapable.

So much for the basis of the genealogy. There now follows the full history of the Linwood Family from its earliest known emergence. The name is first encountered in the middle of the 17th century when the will of Gilbert Linwood was deposited at Northampton in 1641. It also had a variant, which appears as 'Lynwood' in Administrations, or details of the management of an state of a deceased person by an executor, of *circa* 1677 to 1705 and again in 1710. The first Matthew, the husband of Elizabeth—her surname is not known, was a prosperous farmer at Ecton (the village from which Benjamin Franklin's family originated) near Cogenhoe (pronounced 'Cookno') five miles east of Northampton.

In 1660, Matthew **i** purchased the rights of Lord of the Manor in the Wymersley Hundred from one Bond, to whom the Cheyne Family, who had held the hereditary rights since the 12th century, sold it in 1600. This Matthew, the progenitor of his line, died in 1674 and his will was proved in July of that year. His son was Matthew **ii** who married Elizabeth Page, and whose dates of birth and death are not known, but whose youngest son, Richard, was born in 1704 and was residing at Bedford in 1738. His eight children included three daughters and five sons, of whom the eldest, John, had been awarded a Bachelor of Arts degree at Oxford but died young in 1679. The heir, therefore, was Matthew **iii**, who was baptised in 1693 and married Martha Whalley in 1723. She was the sister of Peter Whalley, a Fellow of St. John's College, Oxford, who became the Rector of St. Peter's Church, Cogenhoe, when, in 1723, he purchased the 'advowson', or the right to appoint or select the incumbent of the church. The Rectorate passed first to his son, Bradley Whalley, who presented a silver coffee pot to the Church to be sold and the proceeds used to purchase a communion flagon. This is by Henry Brind, London, 1743, and is mentioned by Christopher A. Markham in his *The Church Plate of the County of Northampton*. The Rectorate then passed to Peter Whalley's grandsons.

Matthew **iii** died in 1782 and his widow, Martha, in 1784. His son, Matthew **iv**, the first silversmith of the family, was born in July 1726, and married Hannah Meredith of Castle Bromwich Hall, near Birmingham. She was born in 1724. It will be noted that his first registered mark in the **'A'** Book at the Birmingham Assay Office (see mark No. 1) states him to be a 'silversmith' whereas in fact he was only a 'plater', like his brothers William and John, that is to say, he coated copper with silver, in exact imitation of the Sheffield craftsmen in the same medium. Subsequently, he became a partner of John Turner, an active silversmith in Birmingham, joining that firm in 1779, when he was 53 years of age.

William Linwood's 'plate-mark' (struck in imitation of the silversmiths' hallmarks) was first registered under a clause which had been inserted into the Act of 1773 (for the establishment of Assay Offices at Birmingham and Sheffield) whereby platers were permitted to imitate a portion of the 'hallmark' providing they paid a penalty of £100, but in spite of this 'fine', the Guardians of the Sheffield Assay Office insisted on the 'registration' of all Birmingham platers. William's mark, therefore, consisted of his name and an 'ostrich feather', and was, like his brother John's mark—an 'oak tree'—registered in 1807. Matthew **iv**'s second registered mark in the **'A'** Book at Birmingham, where he is described as a 'plater', must have been entered after 1784, when the above clause was first introduced, because the marks are in the **'A'** Book, and presumably had been first registered at Sheffield, since it is inconceivable that the latter would have permitted the use of an unregistered punch, or that the former would have entered such into their own register.

To return to the genealogy: Matthew **iv** died at Leicester in 1783, and his widow, Hannah, in 1805. He had moved to Leicester from Birmingham. In her latter years, Hannah resided with her famous daughter, Mary Linwood, in the latter's home in London at Belgrave Square. Both Matthew **iv** and Hannah were buried in St. Margaret's Church, Leicester. As has been said above, they had seven children, of whom Matthew **v** was the eldest; he was born in 1754. His sister, Mary the embroideress was born in 1755 (not 1756 as stated in the pamphlet mentioned above) and his brothers William and John were born in 1756 and 1760 respectively. His younger sister, Sarah, who was born in 1759 married Samuel Markland in 1798. He also had two other sisters named Ann and Harriet but nothing further is known of them.

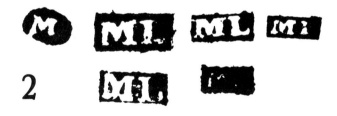

Mary Linwood was baptised at Leicester in 1756. Showing early promise, she eventually established an academy where young ladies were taught the craft of needlework, and herself attained a great mastery of the art. Her work consisted mainly of needlework pictures in coloured worsteds, which were copies of paintings by Morland, Northcote, and even Raphael. A contemporary engraving of 1805 reveals Miss Linwood to have been a stately lady with average features. Her work received Royal recognition, and Queen Charlotte's 'encouraging behaviour' led to an exhibition of her work at the Pantheon, Oxford Street. One of her masterpieces—a portrait of Napoleon—is in the Textile Room of the Victoria and Albert Museum. She died in 1845 and is also buried at St. Margaret's, Leicester.

Matthew **v** was the 'Boxmaker', although his son, the last Matthew, probably helped him until, in 1815, he left Birmingham for London. Matthew **v** was apprenticed to one Joseph Hunt, but the date of his apprenticeship is not known; he would have been twelve or thirteen years of age at the time, so this would be *circa* 1766-7, before the Birmingham Assay Office was opened, and Hunt was probably registered at Chester as a 'smallworker' (he is not recorded in Jackson). Joseph Hunt, or his son, as this could be yet another case of both father and son sharing the same Christian name) was working as late as 1818, where he is described in a directory as a 'Gilt Toy, Plated Military and Crest Button Maker', and is recorded again, in 1839, as a 'Steel Toy Maker'. The apprenticeship fee which Matthew **v** paid was £48, which was an appreciable sum in those days; Matthew **v** was not apprenticed to his father, as *his* son Matthew **vi** was, because Matthew **iv** was not a real silversmith, having, as stated above, joined John Turner's firm at 24, Great Charles Street in 1779 as a partner. This firm, according to Mr. Arthur Westwood's paper read to the *Birmingham Archaeological Society* in 1904, was of a considerable size, and made small silver wares, such as snuffboxes, clasps, seals and buckles of various kinds. John Turner was one of the thirty Guardians named in the Assay Act of 1773, and on retiring from business in *circa* 1781, he was appointed a Warden, in which office he served a term of one year.

Matthew **v**'s first mark was entered in the **'A'** Book at Birmingham in 1813, but he had been appointed a Guardian of the Assay in 1811. His second mark was entered in 1820, and he retired from business in 1822. He died in 1826. His wife was Frances Giles (probably the daughter of one Joseph Giles, a chaser and engraver, who lived at Snow Hill). She died in 1837. As far as can be ascertained, there was only one child of this marriage, and he was Matthew **vi**, who was born in 1783. He married Susanna—(her surname is unknown) who died in 1834. They lost their infant son and daughter in 1815, while they lived at St. Paul's Square, and after this tragedy, went to live in London, where Linwood opened a jeweller's shop in Fleet Street, where he probably sold his father's wares. He lived in Hoxton Old Town, and died in 1847. He was buried in the churchyard of St. Mary's, Haggerston, in

3

the then Haggerston Ward of Shoreditch. This building was bombed in the Second World War, and when the ruins were cleared, a giant housing estate was erected on the spot. Thus, like the Pembertons in the vault of the Old Meeting House in Birmingham before him, the last of the Linwoods, silversmiths supreme, lies under a mass of bricks and mortar.

Matthew Linwood **v**'s workshop produced some of the finest of all the Birmingham boxes. Again, like the other boxmakers discussed in these genealogies, he must have had many skilled workers, but none have been recorded. His memorial, like theirs, is the beauty and ingenuity of his craftsmanship.

The Mills Family

As far as may be ascertained, the Mills family sprang from pure yeoman roots. There is nothing to indicate otherwise than that the firm was begun in 1767 by Joseph Mills, who, to judge from his date of birth (his obituary notice in Aris's *Birmingham Gazette* stated him to be in his 84th year at his death in 1819, thus he was born in 1735) might have been the elder brother of Nathaniel **i** (both he, and his son Nathaniel **ii** will henceforth be distinguished by the use of bold numerals) who was born in 1746. The name of Joseph Mills first occurs in Sketchley's *Birmingham Directory* of 1767. There is no direct evidence that Joseph and Nathaniel **i** were related, but as there are no other 'Mills' in the Directories of the period, nor can any be found in other sources, this relationship is probable. Joseph is described in the Directory as a 'silversmith and publican', which seems an odd combination, but other similar entries have been noted where two professions, one slightly more imposing than the other, have been followed. In any case, it is very probable that the designation 'silversmith' covers nothing more than a back-street repairer of broken buckles and other trivia.

Nathaniel Mills, the elder, was born (where, is not stated) in 1746. He married twice. Neither of his wives' names are known, but the first died in 1804, after an apparently childless marriage. His second wife bore him six children, of whom Nathaniel **ii** was the second. The date of her death is not known, but their youngest son, John, died aged only 26 in 1850, so she must have been alive until 1824 at least. Nathaniel **i** appears in Pye's *Birmingham Directory* in 1790 as a 'Jeweller' of Church Street, and again in 1797, this time at 2 Northwood Street. The Mills' were to live in this street, at one time or another, for the next sixty years.

The first mention of Nathaniel **i** as a silversmith comes in the **'A'** Book of the Birmingham Assay Office, that is, the first Register commencing 1773 when the Assay Office was first opened. The

firm, entered in 1803, was a partnership between Mills and one Langston, of whom nothing more is known. It is probable, though by no means certain, that Mills, being a jeweller rather than a manufacturer by profession, took Langston as a working partner —the one making the articles, the other providing the finance and selling them—until he had learned enough of the trade to employ his own apprentices. The fact that Mills does not appear as an apprentice anywhere in the records, might indicate this. The practice of financing a company of silversmiths is not limited to Mills. Matthew Boulton, also, was a contractor rather than an actual silversmith, and one of the six 'Matthew Linwoods' (Matthew **iv**) joined John Turner in 1779 when he was 53 years of age, hardly the time for an apprenticeship. Similarly, Mills in 1803 was 57 years old, so the indications are that he *was* the financier of the company at this early stage.

1

2

It is not known what type of articles this partnership produced, as none have been encountered, but it is highly probable that small items such as buckles (which were then at the height of fashion) and vinaigrettes might have been made. Their joint mark was entered at the Assay Office, and, as will be noted (see Mark No. 1) consisted of the letters **ML** enclosed in an elongated punch. This could, at first glance, be mistaken for one of the Linwood marks, except that, on closer examination, the 'serifs' or tails of the letters, are more pronounced on the former—the top serif of the letter **L** in particular—and could thus serve to distinguish the two. As may be seen from the photograph, the mark is quite tiny, not more than $\frac{1}{8}$ of an inch long, but the Linwood marks are even smaller, so no great confusion should arise here if they are carefully scrutinised. It must be pointed out, however, that the enlarged marks are ten times larger than life, and some even larger, and will not appear on articles in this size.

Nathaniel **i**'s family consisted of 3 sons and 3 daughters. Of these, the eldest was Elizabeth, born in 1807, who died in 1854 aged 47, still a spinster. One of the other daughters, Sarah, married one Gordon, but nothing more is known of her. Nathaniel **ii**, the silversmith who produced all the superlative boxes, was born in 1811, and was presumably apprenticed to his father; he would have been working from about 1830. The first mention of a son in the company is found in Chapman's *Birmingham Directory* of 1841, where the firm appears as 'N. Mills & Son, Caroline Street', and again in 1845 (after Nathaniel **i**'s death, which was in 1840) as 'N. Mills & Sons'. This was strictly misleading as Nathaniel **ii**'s sons in 1845 were tiny infants, but it served him to thus designate himself.

Nathaniel **i** lived to the hale old age of 93, so it must be presumed that he must have retired long before his death in 1840. It seems certain that Nathaniel **ii** succeeded him and with this infusion of new ideas and techniques, the firm prospered. It will be noted that all the cast and 'repoussé-top' boxes and vinaigrettes stem from this post-1830 period, primarily because new methods were introduced, as has been stated in the section on 'Repoussé and Embossing', but also because the Birmingham manufacturers in general, and Nathaniel **ii** in particular, seized the opportunity of producing 'mass-manufactured articles' at a time when everything was made by hand, and thereby reduced the cost to the retailer, while also benefiting themselves.

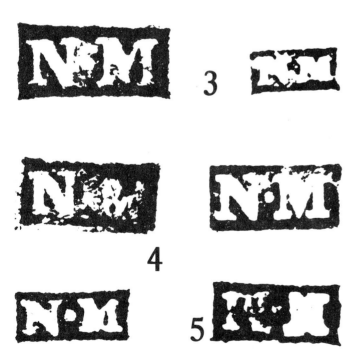

Nathaniel **ii**'s wife, Elizabeth—her surname is unknown—was born in 1816 and died in 1897 at the age of 81. She thus survived her husband (who died in 1873 aged 62) by 24 years. She probably had a fairly comfortable life—Nathaniel **ii** was a rich man and left £30,000 in his will (which sum was a great deal in those days

of low prices) but she had known tragedy: as has been stated above, her infant sons, Frank, aged 3 years, and Frederick William, aged 10 months, had succumbed to Scarlatina in 1848. Her son, John Alfred, who was appointed joint trustee in his father's will providing he reached the age of 21, did not reach his majority. The other trustee was Henry Leerhoff Muller, a German engineer who lived at Edgbaston and who had married Mills' eldest daughter, Emily Maria. Yet a third substitute trustee appears in the will: this is George Smith, whose relationship with Nathaniel is nebulous—he does not appear to have been another son-in-law, although his wife, Elizabeth, was left a sum of money in the will. He was a 'Scot's Snuffbox maker', which presumably refers to the industry at Mauchline in Ayrshire, which was long noted for its treen snuffboxes, made from plane wood or sycamore. The *Jury Report* of the Great Exhibition, dealing with this product, states: 'Mr. W. Chambers states that this is the timber used at Old Cumnock (the centre where these articles were made before Mauchline developed) and that a piece of rough wood which costs 25s. will make snuffboxes to the value of £3000' (Chambers' *Gazeteer of Scotland*).

Elizabeth's youngest son, Allen Gordon, was still living in 1897, and was left a sum of money in his mother's will, but he either emigrated or died intestate, and no further trace of him could be found, in spite of a most careful search, which failed to reveal either the place or the date of his death.

Nathaniel **i**'s will is at Lichfield, where all Staffordshire legal documents were deposited before 1858; after that time, they were stored at Birmingham. He left £1500 and 7 leasehold tenements in Hall Street, 3 dwelling houses in Bread Street, and 'one other, which is a tavern in Bread Street—The Rose'. His executors were Nathaniel **ii** and William Harley, Snuffer Maker of Bartholomew Street, Birmingham. He died on the 11th of January, 1840 and the will was probated on May the 6th, 1840. His signature on the will appears as 'Nath. Mills' in a shaky, but careful, workman's hand. Nathaniel **ii**'s signature on *his* will is in a flowing Victorian Calligrapher's script. He bequeathed to the Trustees the capital and stock in trade of 'N. Mills & Co. Merchants', and stocks and shares and a freehold house in George Street, Aston Manor, plus £350 per annum to his wife for the rest of her natural life.

The silversmithing business appears in Birmingham Trade Directories until 1855 (see Mark No. 5). In 1856 a new designation appears in Francis White & Co.'s *General Directory of Birmingham*: 'Nathaniel Mills, Hardware Commission Merchant. 25 Mary Ann Street. House: 25 George Street, Lozells'. The workshop in 1855 was at 11½ Howard Street, and one could be forgiven for assuming that Mills had gone bankrupt or was otherwise impoverished, whereas, in fact, having decided that silversmithing was too much for him, at the age of 44, he turned to something easier, and possibly, more profitable.

In 1836, the workshop was at 42 Caroline Street, which is still standing today. The house is today used as a warehouse and offices and goes back about fifty yards. It has a Georgian front door and two upper stories with four windows in each and a sloping roof. The house was carefully examined for traces of old workings, but if these exist, they are well hidden. It is interesting that after 1858, No. 42 Caroline Street was first taken over by Thomas Morris, gilt jewellery manufacturer, and then in 1864, by George Unite, Joseph Willmore's apprentice. The last Mills workshop before 11½ Howard Street had been at 72 Northwood Street, so Mills had returned to his father's old haunts.

Nathaniel Mills **ii** died at his son-in-law's house at Grosvenor Road, Hardswarre, in the West Bromwich district of Staffordshire, on the 27th of February, 1873. He and his wife Elizabeth are buried at Key Hill Cemetery and their memorial is a simple marble column topped with an urn. With Nathaniel Mills died a splendid craft which all the coarse confections of the late Victorian era could not possibly emulate.

In conclusion, it should be stated that no amount of dedicated research could uncover any traces of either apprentices or 'outworkers' who were employed by the Mills' workshop, but these must have existed as the output over the years was enormous. Perhaps one day something will come to light which will illuminate this enigma. For the present, this first biography of the Mills Family of Birmingham will have to suffice.

The Willmore Geneaology

Like the Mills family, this line appears to originate from pure yeoman stock, as before 1773, when he entered his mark at the Birmingham Assay Office in partnership with James Alston, nothing appears about the founder of the firm, Thomas Willmore **ii**, in contemporary literature. Alston, a native of North Berwick, worked as a boy under Samuel Garbett, a partner of the celebrated inventor, Dr. John Roebuck, who was associated with James Watt in his early days. Alston was one of the Assay Guardians and a Warden for many years. Their shop was in Colemore Row, and the works, where they produced small articles such as buckles, buttons and seals, was in Suffolk Street.

Thomas **i**, of whose marriage nothing can be traced, died in 1818. He had three sons, but it is not known which one was senior to which: Edward, described in his will as a 'Taylor', who died a bachelor in 1814, John, who married Sarah — and had a family of six children. He was a builder and died in 1816, and Thomas **ii**, who is designated a 'gentleman' in his will, whose first wife's name is unknown, but whose second, Jane Male (the mother of James Male, Solicitor) gave him seven children. Thomas **ii** died in 1816 and his widow in 1831.

John Willmore's eldest son, Joseph **i** was an engineer by profession, inventing a method for making nails in 1808, is described in his father's will as a 'plane maker', that is, he produced tools for working in wood and metal, and on his Death Certificate as a 'Gun Barrel Borer'. He was born in 1792 and married Susanna — who died in 1868. She gave him one daughter, Ann, who married William Evans, a coal merchant. Joseph **i** died in 1865. Another of John's children, Mary Ann, married her cousin, Joseph Willmore **ii**, the silversmith, and died in childbirth in 1848.

The third son of Thomas **i**, namely, Thomas **ii** had, as has been said, seven children. Of these, Joseph **ii** was the subject of this genealogy. He was born in 1790, and was probably apprenticed to his grandfather. He entered his mark in the '**A**' Book at the Birmingham Assay Office about 1808 (the entry is rather vaguely dated, but other marks which were entered in 1808 are adjacent) when he was 18 years old. In 1810, he took the young George Unite (the name is written 'Unitt' in the Indenture) the son of Samuel Unitt of Birmingham, as an apprentice. The elder Unitt is described in the Indenture as a 'Gilt Toymaker' of Birmingham. Unitt Junior, was then aged 12 years, and was to receive the sum of 3/- per week and his keep, the sum increasing by 6d. per annum until his Freedom was attained in 1818.

Joseph Willmore **ii** married his cousin Mary Ann, but it is not known in which year. She died in childbirth at the age of 40. They do not appear to have had any other children. On her Death Certificate, Mary Ann is described as the wife of Joseph Willmore, 'Glass Toy Maker', which is one of the many professions which the Birmingham silversmiths pursued. Indeed, Kelly's *Post Office Directory* for the year in which he died, 1855, lists him under the heading of 'Glass Bead and Gilt Toy Maker', and states his home to be 72 Sumner Lane, but on the Death Certificate of his wife, the address is given as '117 Summer Lane [sic] which is probably an error by the clerk.

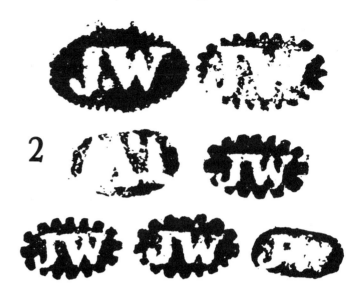

2

Office. These were entered between 1832 and 1834, and in the latter year, John Yapp and John Woodward were taken as partners, although the mark still showed only Willmore. Another mark was entered in 1835, which was probably Willmore's last mark, and this appears to have a plain outline. Willmore entered his mark at the London Assay Office also. He first registered a mark in 1808 while he had a showroom in Bouverie Street, and secondly in 1823 when he was at Thavies Inn, Holborn. Joseph Willmore retired from business in 1851 and lived until his death in 1855 at Withwood Cottage, King's Norton in Worcestershire. He was buried in Key Hill Cemetery, Birmingham. His will has not been traced.

The remaining children of Thomas **ii** included William, who was a Scavenger by trade, that is, he collected refuse from private dwellings, and lived at Clerkenwell, London, and who died in 1853, George Edwin, who died aged 25 in 1831, and Samuel, who was still a minor when his father's will was probated in 1816.

Joseph Willmore was a superlative silversmith, who worked in the Trade for almost half a century. His was no 'bought-in' partnership, but skill acquired by hard work. Although, with the exception of George Unite, who was himself to become a fine craftsman, no other apprentices can be traced, this manufactory must have numbered some splendid craftsmen on its staff, and the quality of the embellishment (even if the articles were sent to 'outworkers') indicates Willmore's preoccupation with fine workmanship. Some of the finer 'shapes', mostly vinaigrettes, were produced in Willmore's workshop, but he also made other small articles such as salt-spoons, caddy-spoons, wine labels, buckles and buttons, as well as, of course, the exceptionally fine snuffboxes with or without cast or repoussé scenes upon the lids.

His former partners, Yapp and Woodward, entered their first mark as independent silversmiths in May, 1845, but with Joseph Willmore's death, the silversmithing connection died also.

1

As will be seen from Mark No. 1, Joseph's first mark was **JW** in a rectangular punch, but Jackson, page 409, illustrates a mark identified as that of Joseph Willmore and dated 1805, which is in an oval punch with a plain edge, not the characteristic 'serrated edge' of the later Willmore punches. Where he obtained this ascription is not known.

Joseph Willmore entered two series of marks at the Assay

3

Joseph Taylor

Unlike the previous personalities whose names are sufficiently unusual as to render research into their genealogies somewhat easier—even the Mills' are not very common in Warwickshire and Staffordshire—there are hundreds of 'Taylors' in the Probate Registers and other contemporary sources, and the isolation of suitable material is made well-nigh impossible. There was, it is true, an obituary notice in Aris's *Birmingham Gazette* of the 16th of July, 1827 which stated: 'On Tuesday, after a few hours illness, in the 60th year of his age, Mr. Joseph Taylor of Newhall Street', but until documentary evidence was forthcoming, this person might have been anyone.

Wills are, of course, extremely valuable factors in any genealogy, and fortunately Joseph Taylor made his in February 1816; it is in the Probate Division of Somerset House, and immediately the document was read, the nebulous position changed. Although there is not a great deal of information, such as there is constitutes entirely new material, and is therefore of great interest here. The will commences: 'This is the last will and testament of one Joseph Taylor of Birmingham in the County of Warwick *Silversmith*', and with this designation, the hunt is over. There is, of course, no account of Taylor's antecedents (nor are any available from other sources) but his next of kin are named: his

page 408, line 12, ascribed to him as of '1787'. As may be further noted (see Mark No. 2), Taylor entered one version of his famous '**IT** in an oval' in 1813, the year in which he was appointed a Guardian of the Assay, but there was an '**IT** in a rectangular punch' struck the same year.

In common with most of the silversmiths discussed in these genealogies, Taylor's apprentices are not known, but he must have employed some superb artists, as his boxes, the cast specimens in particular, are quite outstanding. In this connection, it is interesting that one of the early entries in the '**A**' Book is one for 'Levy Perry' (whose mark was '**LP** in an oval') who entered in 1777, and who made instrument cases, boxes and buttons, and who worked at 20 Bartholomew Chapel. This was probably John Perry Senior's father. John Perry Senior himself was also named in Taylor's will, and was, of course, his sister's father-in-law, so it could be that John Perry, Junior, coming as he did, from silversmithing stock, was an apprentice of Taylor's. It would be entirely natural for him to marry his master's sister, and by this means, Joseph Taylor, who had begun his working life making watch-cases, was able to reinforce his workshop with skilled craftsmen.

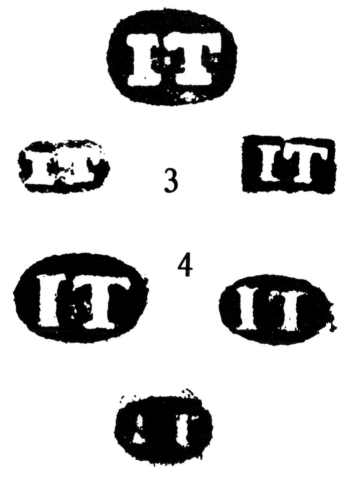

brother John and sister Dorothy, and his children, Joseph William, Amelia Franks, and Sophia Taylor. An obituary announcement also in Aris's *Birmingham Gazette* dated the 3rd of February 1812, states: 'On Saturday last, in the 43rd year of her age, Mrs. Taylor, wife of Mr. Joseph Taylor of Newhall Street, in this town', so the daughters could not have been very old when the will was made.

Joseph Taylor's sister, Dorothy, married John Perry the Younger, and he, and his brother Charles (who is designated a 'dealer in metals') are appointed joint executors with Joseph's brother John. When it is remembered that the '**A**' Book in the Birmingham Assay Office contains the partnership mark of Taylor & Perry which is **T & P**, entered in July 1829, it becomes clear that when Joseph died in 1827, his brother John, and his son-in-law, John Perry, succeeded to his business. They were both left substantial sums in the will (Taylor left £18,000 altogether) and his premises and goods in both Birmingham and London. Joseph Taylor had a shop or showroom in Bouverie Street, off Fleet Street, and his Trade Card, in addition to a somewhat enigmatic elephant browsing in the foliate background (possibly symbolic of the ivory which Taylor sold), has a splendid memorial, on which are engraved his name and trade, and which is guarded over by an angel and a cherub on either side. The text reads: 'J. Taylor, Working Gold and Silversmith, Jeweller, Tortoiseshell and Ivory Box, Gilt and General Toy Manufacturer, 35 Newhall Street, Birmingham, and 2 Bouverie Street, Fleet Street, London'. The whole is surmounted by the Arms of the London Goldsmiths' Company, and the card was engraved by Francis Eginton.

Very little, almost nothing at all, is known of Joseph Taylor's early life. To judge from his somewhat crabbed signature, he was not of patrician stock as were Pemberton and Linwood, and therefore early evidence is not forthcoming. All that can be firmly stated is that he entered his first mark while he was at Aston, near Birmingham, and that it was a 'watchmaker's punch', that is to say, he made watch-cases, (like many other small-workers) which were stamped with two separate letters, not in a rectangular punch as on larger items. His second mark, entered *circa* 1790, was, as may be seen, a primitive **IT** in a ragged cut-corner rectangular punch, and not the '**IT** in an oval' which Jackson,

Modern hand engraved copper plaque: especially commissioned to illustrate the process, pioneered by Mills, of hand engraving on an engine-turned ground. The choice of the Post Office Tower in London is deliberate, to show the way in which a contemporary subject would have been treated.

This article made in collaboration by two Birmingham craft workshops.

Makers: Messrs. F. L. Lancaster and V. Joliffe, Birmingham 1968.

Size: 4 inches by 3¼ inches.